PACKIN' UP AND HEADIN' OUT

PACKIN' UP AND HEADIN' OUT

Making the Most of Your College Adventure

Jill and John Bowling

Beacon Hill Press of Kansas City
Kansas City, Missouri

Copyright 2001
by Beacon Hill Press of Kansas City

ISBN 083-411-8998

Printed in the
United States of America

Cover Design: Kevin Williamson

Library of Congress Cataloging-in-Publication Data

Bowling, Jill, 1948-
  Packin' up and headin' out : making the most of your college adventure / Jill and
John Bowling.
    p. cm.
  ISBN 0-8341-1899-8 (pbk.)
    1. College student orientation—United States—Handbooks, manuals, etc. 2. Col-
lege students—United States—Life skills guides. I. Title: Packing up and heading
out. II. Bowling, John C., 1949- III. Title.

LB2343.32 .B69 2001
378.1'98—dc21

                                                              2001025512

10   9   8   7   6   5   4   3   2   1

This book is dedicated to Brian Parker and the entire Admissions staff of Olivet Nazarene University, Bourbonnais, Illinois, whose tireless work has helped thousands of students make a successful transition from high school to college.

CONTENTS

PREFACE

Congratulations! You have completed high school and have been admitted to college. Way to go. You may not realize it, but you are privileged. The percentage of Americans who actually go to college after high school is not as high as you might think. Just getting into college gives you a head start in terms of your potential for success and personal development. Go ahead, pat yourself on the back.

As you begin packing your clothes and other necessities, it is also important for you to prepare emotionally, mentally, and spiritually for the demands you are about to face. During the next few years, you will be challenged in nearly every area of your life. Personally, you have to accept great responsibility for your life. Academically, you will be stretched and pressured like never before. This will also be a time during which you will meet lots of new people and develop some lifelong friendships. Your college/university years should also give you the time and opportunity to let your faith mature and develop.

We are privileged to live and work on a college campus. We have seen thousands of students come and go. We have laughed and cried, cheered and prayed with hundreds of them. From our vantage point, we can see that your days in college may be the *most significant time in your life*. The scores of decisions you will make during these years will have a forever impact on your life.

We have also seen how important it is for a student to get off to a good start. *Packin' Up and Headin' Out* is for students making the transition from high school to college. Each section introduces you to some of the issues you will face during your first few months on campus.

This book doesn't have all the answers, but it does ask the right questions and points you in the right direction.

As you begin college, start with a sense of excitement, confidence, and a strong determination to succeed. Be assured that "he who began a good work in you will carry it on to completion" (Phil. 1:6).

We wish you well!

Part 1

THE COLLEGE ADVENTURE

To learn is to change. Education is a process that changes the learner.
—George Leonard

Moving into New Territory

Did you know that half of all the freshmen who start college this fall will never receive a degree? About one-third of this year's freshman class will not reach their sophomore year. So, making a successful transition from high school to college may be more important than you think.

And what you may need to know more than anything else is this: *The key to a great college experience is not where you go, but who you are.* Your success in this adventure called college will depend in great measure on your ability to come to grips with the issues presented in this book.

The good news is—you can succeed in college and have a great time doing it. However, that won't just happen naturally, and it won't all be easy.

The transition from high school to college brings with it an array of challenges and opportunities. This is one of the great *passages* of life. Although four years in college seems like a long time when you are just starting out, a college career is relatively brief when measured against the entire span of your life. But the impact of these years is immense and perhaps more dramatic and significant that any other period in life.

Why? Because during these years, besides getting an education that will provide you with an academic foundation for life, you will also

- make the transition from living at home to living on your own
- move from being under the nearly constant authority and supervision of your parents to being independent
- choose a career path
- develop lifelong friendships
- more formally establish your personality
- and you may find a life mate

You have a lot at stake in these years. Getting off to the right start is vital. So let's take just a moment for . . .

A WORD ABOUT YOUR FEET

You may already realize the fact that the foot is a remarkable and intricate part of the human body. A person's foot holds 26 bones, 33 joints, 107 ligaments, 19 muscles, and various tendons that hold the composition together and let it move in various ways. Some folks have big feet, others have petite feet, most are somewhere in between. *And* a pair of feet includes 250,000 tiny sweat glands that excrete as much as a half a pint of moisture each day. (OK, that fact may be a little more than you want to know.)

But you do need to know that your feet will be important to you as you head off to college. They will take you wherever you go on campus. They are with you in class, in the dorm room, and in the dining hall. They go with you on your dates and when you play ball; they are with you in the shower or at church.

Have you ever thought about how many figures of speech relate to your feet? Can you think of any? Here are a few:

We speak of . . .

putting our *best foot forward*

gaining a *foothold*

being *footloose*

or having *two left feet*

the *foot of the bed* (Do beds have feet?)

You will soon be *getting your feet wet* at college. You will have the chance to *sit at the feet* of some great teachers. Throughout the semester they may ask that your term papers have a series of *footnotes.* You will want to be sure to *get off on the right foot* with your professors, so you don't end up *dragging your feet* on the assignments. You see, if you don't *toe the line*, the prof may have to *put his or her foot down.*

One popular movie a few years ago was *Runaway Bride* with Richard Gere and Julia Roberts. It's the story of a woman who keeps backing out of getting married. She gets *cold feet,* right?

Evidently she's afraid to commit, afraid of the unknown. She becomes immobilized by her fear of the unknown and ends up running away.

That happens in real life from time to time, and occasionally it happens to students who become overwhelmed by all of the demands thrust upon them as they pack up and head off to college.

Whether you look at the next four years with excitement or dread, realize almost everyone is filled with anxiety during the first few weeks of college. Facing the unknown isn't easy. Regardless of where you go to school and what you study, one thing is sure—the decision to attend college will mean some major changes in your life. But you don't have to get cold feet. Just take a deep breath and take one step at a time.

All first-year students face issues such as wondering if they will fit in or if they will be able to find their way around campus or if they can compete academically. You don't need to let those things throw you. As you start, just be aware of some . . .

FUNDAMENTAL DIFFERENCES BETWEEN HIGH SCHOOL AND COLLEGE

First of all, you simply face more demands when you go to college. You not only have to balance the requirements of the academic program but also have to come to grips with all of the issues involved in being on your own.

You have more freedom and fewer restrictions—*but* with the freedom comes more responsibility.

College brings more opportunities to explore academic and personal interests.

Regardless of the courses you take in college, you will probably notice a change in the academic workload. Course work will increase in both the amount of work required and the difficulty (or at least complexity) of the material. Plan on spending more time on schoolwork than you did in high school.

Although most colleges have a set number of general education requirements (certain courses everyone has to take), you will have more freedom in setting up your weekly schedule of courses. Getting the right courses in the right sequence will be your responsibility.

Socially, you are once again at "the bottom of the totem pole." That is both good and bad. The tough part is that you suddenly go from being among the oldest and most knowledgeable students, to being among the group of students who don't have it all figured out yet.

The good part of starting over is that you do have the opportunity to start over, to shed some of the baggage you may have accumulated through mistakes you made in high school. Going to college gives you the chance to begin again.

You have a clean slate—academically and socially. Make the most of it!

If you want to make the most of your college adventure, you will need a good measure of self-discovery and self-discipline. You may have to balance added freedom with some initial lack of direction. You may experience the simultaneous joy of new friends along with the sadness of missing your friends from home. Nearly every aspect of your life will experience some measure of change.

As this happens, it is important for you to face the natural changes that come with going to college, accept them (even if you don't enjoy them), and begin to use change as a way to move you toward your goals.

To succeed in college, you must be able to manage change and use it as an avenue through which you can discover yourself, accept your strengths and limitations, and challenge yourself to be the best you can be.

Your freshman year is vital to the success of your whole college experience. Not only does your first year comprise one-fourth of your college experience, but also during this year you will establish patterns, priorities, and habits that will set the pace for the rest of your college career.

Successful Beginnings

As you begin to think about your transition from high school to college, consider these . . .

Four Keys to Success

Start with the end in mind. Your destination will determine your direction. In Lewis Carroll's story *Alice in Wonderland,* Alice faces a moment when she is temporarily lost and comes to a crossroad not knowing which way to go. Alice sees the Cheshire Cat in a tree and asks him which way she should go. He replies, *"Where are you going?"*

"I'm not quite sure," she says.

"Well, then, it doesn't matter which road you take," the cat notes.

Decide now where you are headed. Clarify your goals. Make sure you have thought it through. Do you have a clear picture in your mind of where you are going and what you will need to do to get there?

When college begins, you will face hundreds of decisions, and each will shape your future. Such decision making requires a clear picture of the overall goals of your life and of your time at college. When you learn to set goals and begin to do the things that will make those goals come true, you will discover wonderful new joy and energy and fulfillment.

To achieve the most in life you must have a clear picture of what you want.

Why are you going to college?

_____
_____
_____
_____
_____
_____

What do you think the ideal college experience should be? _____

_____
_____
_____
_____
_____

Where do you want to be four years from now?

_____
_____
_____
_____
_____

Where do you want to be when you are 25 or 30?

_____
_____
_____
_____
_____

Having a plan in mind as you begin college can help you structure the unknown and set you free. Often people who feel overwhelmed, unfulfilled, or even depressed are those who have no dream or vision to sustain them. With clearly defined goals and carefully chosen action plans, you increase the probability that you'll get what you want out of college and out of life.

As you begin to plan, your focus is improved and your activities and energies begin to work together to make your plan a reality. And remember it's OK to change your plan as time passes. Setting goals doesn't lock you in for life. In fact, just the opposite happens—you begin to experience a new freedom that comes from a clear picture of why you are attending college and what you want to accomplish. By starting with the end in mind, you will increase the odds of being successful.

As you choose your goals for the future, be sure that you go beyond just *having* goals, such as:

"I want to *have* a degree."

"I want to *have* a job and a car."

Those goals are fine, but there is more to life than just *having* certain things. Goals should also include *doing*.

"I want to exercise regularly."

"I want to travel. I want to attend. I want to serve."

These *doing* goals will enrich your life.

You should also have some *being* goals. Who you are (much more than what you have or do) will determine the quality and satisfaction of your life.

Planning doesn't put you in a straitjacket. You can always adjust the plan and choose how you want to go about reaching your goals. Good planning increases your options rather than restricts them.

On the other hand, without a plan you become a victim of circumstances. You react rather than act. You begin to coast—and the only way to coast is to go *downhill!*

Having goals . . .

will give you focus

will call you forward

will stimulate you to action and
will help you persist

Have you heard the story of the three bricklayers who
were all asked what they were doing? The first man answered gruffly, "I'm laying bricks." The second man
replied, "I'm building this wall." But the third man could
see more than the bricks or the wall. He declared, "I'm
building a cathedral."

Goals extend and enrich how you see the daily demands of going to college. You are doing more than "taking a class," more than "getting through the semester."
You are, brick by brick, building your future. So be sure to
start with the end in mind.

**Decide to take full advantage of the support system
in place to help you succeed.** Colleges have everything
students need to reach their goals. When the alarm clock
goes off on the first day and you head to class, you will
find in place, waiting for you, scores of professors who
have earned hundreds of academic degrees from colleges
and universities around the world. Hundreds of different
classes will be offered in many areas of study.

At the heart of every campus is a library/learning resource center with thousands of books, periodicals, elec-
tronic search services and hundred of computers. Every
school has staff members who work in offices, mow
grass, serve meals, clean your rest rooms, sweep hall-
ways, change lightbulbs, maintain the college grounds,
and stay up all night to ensure your safety.

*All this is done for you so you can concentrate on the
main reason you are in school—to get an education.* Take
advantage of everything provided to help you succeed.
Don't look at the reasons why you can't succeed—simply
determine that you will make it.

A few years ago at a college graduation in the Midwest, a graduate was brought to the platform in his wheelchair. He lifted himself up and with the help of a walker made his way across the platform to the school president. After receiving his diploma, he moved a step or two and then fell to the platform floor. The audience gasped and the college president and others turned to help him. But the student said in a strong voice, "I can make it." And he did. He got up by himself and made it the rest of the way to the cheers of the crowd.

You can make it to graduation, if you want it enough. It won't be easy, but it will be worth it.

What do you think will be the hardest part of starting college?

_____

_____

_____

_____

What will be the most enjoyable part of college for you?

_____

_____

_____

_____

Make your choices carefully. You, more than any other person on your campus, will decide what your freshman year will be like. If you think you will like it, you probably will. If you think you can succeed, success will come. During the transition from high school to college, you must come to grips with who you are, what you believe, and what you value. Success begins with you, for the quality of your life will flow from your heart and mind.

Once upon a time an old blind woman lived in a small house just outside of town. Her reputation for wisdom was known far and wide. One day some young people visited the woman, intent on testing her wisdom.

Their plan was this: they would enter her house and

ask her one question they felt she could not answer because of her blindness.

As they stood before her, one of them said: "Old woman, I hold in my hand a bird. Tell me whether it is living or dead."

She did not answer, and the question was repeated, "Is the bird I am holding living or dead?"

Still she did not answer. She could not see her visitors, much less see what was in their hands. She did not know their faces, their names, their color, their gender; she only knew their motive.

The old woman sat silently. Finally she spoke, her voice soft but stern. "I do not know," she said. "I do not know whether the bird you are holding is dead or alive. But I do know that it is in your hands."

She sensed that the bird was alive, but if she said, "The bird is alive," its holder would only have to squeeze a little harder and the bird would be dead.

So she said what alone was true about the bird and the one who held it. She said, "It is in your hands."

When you go to college, your success or failure, to a large degree, is "in your hands." You won't be able to control everything that happens to you, but you can choose how you will respond.

Let God be part of your journey. God must be first in your life, if you will really succeed in college or anything else. God wants you to succeed and wants you to be happy. His intentions for you are good. Too often young people think God wants to spoil their good times and take away their freedom. That couldn't be farther from the truth.

These years of university life should push you to the limits of your ability and, thus, help you grow and mature. If you will accept that challenge, you will find a level of adventure and achievement you have never known before, and you will be prepared for a lifetime of accomplishment. But that is only possible if you let God have His rightful place in your life.

Making God part of your life adds meaning and joy and zest. It's like a white-water experience. In Luke 5 is a story that begins:

> One day as Jesus was standing by the Lake of Gennesaret, with the people crowding around him and listening to the word of God, he saw at the water's edge two boats, left there by the fishermen, who were washing their nets. He got into one of the boats, the one belonging to Simon, and asked him to put out a little from shore. Then he sat down and taught the people from the boat.
>
> When he had finished speaking, he said to Simon, "Put out into deep water, and let down the nets for a catch." (Vv. 1-4)

Like all of Scripture, these words have a specific historic context. This command was given to a particular person, Simon, and it had a particular meaning for him, but these words of Jesus and their application are not limited to a particular time or place.

Therefore, I believe these words to Simon are also God's words for you as you get ready for the transition from high school to college. *"Put out into deep water, and let down the nets for a catch."* As you begin this new adventure, don't hesitate to launch out, as Jesus says, into the deep water and let down your nets for a catch.

You see . . .

Shallow water breeds shallow people.

Shallow water presents no challenge and therefore yields no reward.

Shallow water fosters caution rather than courage.

Shallow water produces superficial thinking.

It yields immature behavior.

It results in only surface relationships.

But deep water brings an abundant catch and produces men and women of depth and character, men and women fit for life.

We should be white-water people, living where the breakers roll and where the surge of the sea unleashes its power and bounty. Don't be content with sand when you could have surf. Launch out personally, academically, socially, and spiritually.

God calls you to launch into the deep, not because He wants you to sink—but because He wants you to swim, and you can't learn to swim in shallow water. So dive in. Go for it. Learn how to learn and learn how to live.

Consider the following quotation from Phil Edwards:

There is a need in all of us for controlled danger. That is, there is a need for activity that puts us on the edge of life, that forces us out into the deep. There are uncounted millions of people right now who are going through life without any sort of real vibrant kick.

Now Phil Edwards, who wrote those words, is not a preacher, he's not a professor, nor a poet, nor a philosopher. He is one of the world's champion surfers. And he is writing about riding a surfboard.

One thing you learn early when you are learning to surf is that you have to get out where the big waves are. You can't ride the board on waves that are ankle deep. You can't spend your time paddling around in the little pools near the shore. If you want to surf, you have to get out where the white water runs. Going deep is the first thing you have to do, if you are going to catch the big wave.

When you paddle a surfboard to where the water is well over your head, you begin to feel the rhythm of the sea. You feel the waves building and you wait for the right wave. You ride just in front of it, at first, and let it lift you. Then, just as it begins to crest, you stand up in one smooth motion, just as if you are standing up on dry ground. You plant your feet firmly on the board.

Then you lean back, just a little, and move the board to the crest where the power is, and suddenly you are riding the wave. It is unbelievable.

You can hear the entire ocean roaring around you. It sounds like 10,000 yards of tearing silk. That tremendous hiss surges under you. The surfboard trembles at your feet. Riding the curl of the wave is a magnificent experience.

On the curl you find power and speed and exhilaration. Those who will launch out in the deep spiritually find a spiritual experience a little like that.

Getting a first-rate education is important, and learning to live in community is vital; but these do not compare to the importance of having a right relationship with God.

Have you accepted Jesus Christ as your Savior and Lord? Have you come to grips with who you are spiritually? This is more than just knowing about God in some vague way. It is knowing God personally. It is committing your life to Christ. This is more than a feeling, a rush of emotion—more than simply being a "cultural Christian" in some kind of generic way. And it is way more than just some long artificial list of dos and don'ts.

Jesus said, "I have come that [you] may have life, and have it to the full" (John 10:10). Abundant living—that's what God wants for you.

Shallow-water people never know abundance. They never know we serve a great and glorious God whose very presence can lift us and propel us forward in exhilarating new ways.

Once in a while when you are surfing, an exceptional wave comes along. If your timing is good, you can crest the curl. Then, coming down the other side, you turn into the wave so that the water itself curls over your head. In that moment, you find yourself in a tunnel of thundering water. It swirls all about you. It's like a whirling cathedral.

The sheet of water above you is so thin that the sunlight glitters like a shower of diamonds cascading around you. And strangely enough, it's very quiet in there and it's peaceful and you can lean back a little as the power of that water lifts and carries you along.

At the end of one of those great days of surfing, you drag yourself and your surfboard onto the beach, ram the board into the sand, fall in front of it, and lean back against it. And the roar of the sea subsides as if to acknowledge the fact that you have won.

The sun, setting on the horizon, cuts itself on the tops of the waves and bleeds across the water right to your feet. You are exhausted, your teeth are loose, and you ache all over—but oh, what a thrill!

It's a magic time. The ride, the risk, the tumbles and spills, the ups and downs have all been worth it, for you have pushed out into the deep and ridden with the waves. But you will never experience that—you will never know what it's like to be swept along in the midst of a watery crystal carriage—until you move into the midst of the waves, until you say yes to all God calls you to be and all He has for you to do.

There are shallow-water people and there are deep-water people. Which will you be?

The world is filled with shallow ones who have carefully planned their lives—everything measured, everything calculated, nothing really risked. They live self-centered lives. They live to get, rather than to give. They spend themselves, little by little, to acquire a collection of things (cars and clothes and all the rest)—things that, in the end, will only rust and fade away.

Don't do that! All of those things are fine, but they are

not enough in themselves. Don't make "getting" the center of your life.

If you stay only in the shallow water, you will have lived a life of mediocrity when you could have given yourself to the deep and risky things of God.

The Bible is filled with great promises you should take with you when you go to college.

"For I know the plans I have for you," declares the LORD, "plans to prosper you and not to harm you, plans to give you hope and a future" (Jer. 29:11).

But seek first his kingdom and his righteousness, and all these things will be given to you as well (Matt. 6:33).

Trust in the LORD with all your heart and lean not on your own understanding; in all your ways acknowledge him, and he will make your paths straight (Prov. 3:5-6).

And we know that in all things God works for the good of those who love him, who have been called according to his purpose (Rom. 8:28).

Be sure to read part 5 of this book, which deals specifically with how to get a fresh start spiritually.

Part 2

THE PERSONAL ADVENTURE

Genuine beginnings begin within us,
even when they are brought to our attention
by external opportunities.
—William Bridges

SEPARATING YOUR PAST FROM YOUR PRESENT

The first few weeks of school will be both exciting and maddening. If you leave home to attend college, you may feel a little displaced. You may feel homesick or even homeless. You'll face a very strong personal dimension to this transition, so get ready.

Very early one morning long before first light, you will cross an imaginary, yet very real line—the line that separates your past from your present.

Once you start college, yesterday is gone forever. It is not forgotten, its influence remains to a certain degree—but those hours will never be yours again. No amount of money can bring them back. No human effort can resurrect yesterday once it is dead.

Crossing this line is, of course, a daily experience. We are always moving from past to present and on to the future. Your life is lived on that narrow thread called "now." But some moments, some days, in the course of life bring this phenomenon a little more into focus. Your first day in college is one of those days. Once you cross the line, you will no longer be defined by your high school experience. College will rule the day.

You are the one, more than any other person, who will determine what kind of year you will have.

Obviously, you can't control everything that may happen to you this first year. No one can. You may have some setbacks—in fact, you probably will. You may encounter a disappointment or two along the way. Life is like that for all of us at times. Yet, generally, you find what you are looking for in life.

If you look for flaws in people, you'll find them. If you look for mistakes, they will be there. If you are looking for trouble, it will surely find you.

But if you look for what is good in others, that's what you'll see. If you look for success rather than failure, generally you will succeed.

The difference is you. Once you get to college, you must decide who you are and where you are going.

DISCOVERING YOURSELF

The ancient Greek philosopher Socrates declared, "The unexamined life is not worth living." For Socrates, the most important issue was to "Know yourself."

At first glance, this issue of knowing yourself seems simple. You only have to make a list:

I am 18 years old.
I live in Atlanta, Georgia.
My name is Julie.
I play the saxophone and soccer.
I want to be a nurse.
I like to ski.
I love pizza.
I have a younger brother.
My folks are divorced, but live in the same town.

On and on the list could go. But there is more to knowing yourself than simply knowing **about** yourself. Deeper issues are at work here and until you come to grips with who you are and what you are going to do with your life . . .

- nothing will satisfy as you thought it might
- nothing will fit as it ought to fit
- no relationship or accomplishment will be able to deliver its intended benefit

Who are you and where are you going? These are foundational questions.

Albert Einstein was once asked what was really vital in mathematics. He turned to the blackboard, erased a set of complicated equations and then wrote: 2 plus 2 equals 4. "That's what's really vital in math," he replied.

Just as the most intricate formulas and math problems are hopeless without a foundation, so are life and learning.

WHO ARE YOU?

The question is not . . .

- Who do people *think* you are?
- Who do you *say* you are?
- Or even, Who do you *want* to be?

But rather, who are you? When the lights are out and no one is around, no one is watching—who are you? To help you answer consider that:

You are more than just a name. The first response most people give to the question, "Who are you?" is their name. That's part of social interaction.

Names are important, no doubt about it.

- We say our names when we meet.
- We sign our names when we write.
- We affix our signatures to legal documents.
- We pass our names along to our children.

Names are important, but you are more than a name. Names only begin the process of defining people—you are a lot more than just your name. You are the person, for good or ill, who defines and gives flesh and substance to your name.

Who are you? You are more than a name . . .

You are more than a genetic code and a physical body. It is true that who you are, in great measure, is the result of a complex string of genetic material that determines everything from your eye color to gender to racial identity and hundreds of other things. And it is true that at the most fundamental level of our genetic makeup, no two living entities will ever be exactly the same. Every individual is truly unique.

This speaks volumes about the uncommon value God places on each person. Everyone is special to God. That is true genetically—but your identity goes beyond that. You are more than your genes.

We can see this perhaps most obviously with identical twins. They may have essentially the same genetic make-up, yet they are different people, for at work in each individual is a "higher order design," which suggests that consciousness, spiritual perception, behaviors, and so on, are also being developed in ways that go beyond genetics.

Who are you? You are more than a name, you are more than a genetic code, and

You are more than the product of your environment. Environment is significant in the development of personality. If you could exchange your life experiences with the person sitting next to you in class, you would be (even with the same genetic makeup as you have now and the same name) a different person. If your life experiences and environment were changed, you would be different—but even so, environment alone does not make you who you are.

Who are you? That's the first question. You are more than a name, more than a genetic code, more than a set of experiences and environmental factors. Who are you?

You are a unique person; you are by creation a child of God. Which means you are

- more than the chance result of a pattern of stimulus and response
- more than a sophisticated animal
- more than just the product of your environment or heredity

You are a person, fashioned, through great mystery, by the God of the universe.

You are a person with free will and the ability to decide, choose, dream, and become.

You are a person created with a spark of the divine within you and you can fan that into flame or smother it with ashes.

You are an individual with a one-of-a-kind mix of characteristics, abilities, aptitudes, desires, and experiences, all of which help determine who you are.

How would you want your college roommate to describe you in a letter to someone else?

_____

_____

_____

_____

_____

_____

One important question is, **Who are you?** The other is, **Where are you going?**

This is, of course, a twofold question —

In a smaller, micro way it means: Where are you going to college? And where do you intend your college career to take you? Why are you going? But those micro questions can't really be answered until you deal with this important question in a macro or larger way:

Where are you going *in your life?*

In her book *Ship of Fools,* Katherine Anne Porter observes: "I'm appalled at the aimlessness of most people's lives today; fifty percent don't pay any attention to where they are going; forty percent are undecided and will go in any direction; only ten percent know what they want, and not even all of them go toward it."

You need to strive for something more. Don't just give in to whatever happens, whatever comes your way.

It is all too easy in this world
- to drift, rather than swim
- to coast when we should pedal
- to walk rather than run

• to wander off, when we should follow

But you can do better!

In reality, you can do only four things with your life.

You can run away from it. That is, you try to avoid responsibility. You don't make the tough decisions; you don't place demands on yourself. Yours is the way of least resistance. You see food and you eat it. You're offered a drink and you drink it. You have a chance for sex and you take it. This is life lived at the lowest common denominator.

The person who runs away from life makes choices—but only by default. This person deals with problems by not dealing with them. If you're like this, you let things slide, you make excuses, you blame others. You run from life. Don't settle for that!

You can run along with it. This approach to life is dominated by "mob" psychology of striving to keep up with your peers and trying to mimic the lives of others about you. Choices are made, but they are made for you, not by you. This is a kind of "living in the third person." Too often people play to an audience that is not really watching. This is the unexamined life, and it is a frustrating, unfulfilling way to live.

So you can run away from life or simply try to run along with it or . . .

You can take hold of it. This is to make your life your own. You live your life so that only your priorities are the driving influence. We can say a lot for this approach to life, but even so, this option, left to its own forces, can quickly become self-centered and narrow in scope.

There is another option, a better option,

You can offer your life. This is the call of the gospel. You can surrender your life to one who is greater than you are. This is the paradox of faith in Christ—you take control of your life by surrendering it to God. You find freedom through your pledge of allegiance to Jesus.

Who are you?

Where are you going?

These personal questions come to the surface in a special way as you transition from high school to college and from dependence to independence.

When you think about your first year at college, what kinds of personal changes do you think you'll have to make?

_____

_____

_____

_____

_____

_____

The Adventure of Managing Your Personal Resources

A person's life is also impacted by the transition to college in relationship to two vital resources—time and money.

Time Management Is Self-Management

I must govern the clock, not be governed by it.
— Golda Meir, former prime minister of Israel

As you start college, take time to take time seriously. College life is one of the busiest times in life as you try to balance your personal life with school, work, and social activities. Time management is very important. Without a planned schedule, you'll probably find yourself always behind, always under pressure, and never really able to do your best.

One intriguing thing about this challenge to manage our time well is that *each person has the same amount of time in the course of a day.* We all have all the time that exists! The most productive person at school has no more time than the one who lets the day pass without accomplishing anything.

We cannot accumulate time like money or stockpile it like raw materials. We are forced to spend it, whether we choose to or not, at a fixed rate of 60 seconds per minute. We cannot turn it on and off. It cannot be replaced—once it is gone it is irretrievable. Nothing is more removed from us than 10 seconds ago. Once time is gone, it is gone forever.

So, although time is limited, our problem is not really time. The problem lies within ourselves. We can't really manage time, we can only *manage ourselves* in relationship to time.

There really is no such thing as "saving time," for you have to spend it. But you can determine, at least in part, *how* you spend it. Every student will have a different time-management approach that works for him or her.

Many schools provide planners students can use to help them manage schedules and assignments. Using a planner is one of the easiest ways to manage time, keep track of assignments, and still have time for friends and recreation.

These steps are important for any planner/organizer to work:

• The first step is to record your assignments as soon as you get them. They may be listed in a syllabus or be given in class.

• Next, estimate the time you will need to complete each assignment

• Then, establish a schedule that indicates when you want to start working on the assignment and when it is due. Start with the due date and work backward. If you have a written assignment due in three weeks, in two weeks you must have accumulated your resources and have started your first draft. In order for that to happen, in the first week (now) you must begin the necessary research.

● Review these assignments and your study schedule regularly. Things will change throughout the semester, and you will need to make adjustments as you go.

Remember that no matter how busy your life was in high school, it will be more hectic after you get underway at college. If you have a few extra moments when you are not in class or studying, use those moments wisely.

Here are some suggestions to make the "in between" moments of your day more productive.

- Make phone calls.
- Check your mail if you are nearby.
- Take care of small housekeeping chores.
- Review your schedule for the day, week, month just to make sure you are still on track.
- Proofread some or all of one of your papers.
- Mail letters.
- Check your E-mail.
- Relax!
- Cluster tasks together. If you have to go somewhere in your car, be sure to run your other errands at the same time.

The secret to time management is to prioritize. You can't do everything, so you must decide what things are most important. *Doing first things first really works.* Your efficiency will go up; your stress will go down.

Sometimes, when things get hectic and we face an overwhelming amount of work and too little time, our first response may be panic and/or paralysis. We sit at our desks staring at the assignment wondering how we will ever finish this.

This is the "I hate my teachers for doing this to me" stage and can get pretty ugly. Like it or not, the only alternative is to get a grip, get a plan, and go to work. One key is to break down a big assignment into smaller, more manageable steps. Sometimes, you will find the assignment isn't quite as big as you thought.

If you do feel totally overwhelmed by an assignment, talk to someone. Talk to your professor or an adviser—someone with the knowledge or authority to help you. You will not be the first person to face that situation.

To maximize your time management recognize and avoid letting these *time-wasters* take too much time
- Poor planning/lack of organization
- Daydreaming
- Perfectionism
- Miscommunication
- Inability to delegate
- Busywork
- Partying
- Snacking
- Drowsiness
- Phone calls
- TV
- Video games
- Computer surfing
- Stopping before an assignment is finished
- Inability to say no
- Interruptions
- Too many commitments

And remember these time tips
- Prioritize.
- Group similar tasks together.
- Prepare ahead.
- Know your "peak" performance periods.
- Establish a regular pattern.
- Learn to say no.

The best time-management techniques in the world can't guarantee you will complete every assignment on time, ace every test, and earn a 4.0 GPA. Time management techniques are only as good as *you* make them. Do the best you can, and then be happy with the results—nobody is perfect.

MONEY MATTERS

I have enough money to last me the rest of my life— unless I buy something.
— Jackie Mason, comedian

Each year college becomes more expensive. Besides working with your financial aid counselor to make sure you can pay your school bill, going to college also means you will have to take more responsibility in managing your money.

The place to begin is to make an estimated list of weekly expenses: gas, entertainment, clothes, toiletries, snacks. Total this amount and add 25 percent. That is what you will probably need on a weekly average. Most college students will find a part-time job to generate the spending money they need. Spend only what you must spend and save the rest—you can always spend it later!

These basic rules will help you:
- Live within your means.
- Develop a budget.
- Beware of cash machines.
- Avoid credit when possible.
- Pay bills on time.
- Save what you can.

College is a great time to learn the skill of money management. It will pay dividends for life.

Going off to college will give you the wonderful opportunity to develop personally. Make sure that as you go, you take with you a clear picture of the kind of person you want to be and . . .

REMEMBER

- Always keep sight of the big picture, *why* you are attending college.

- Set short-term and long-term goals for yourself.
- Be an active student, not a passive one. You are not only responsible but also capable of sailing all the way through the ups and downs of college life.

Part 3
THE ACADEMIC ADVENTURE

Education is what remains when one has forgotten everything he learned in school.
—Albert Einstein

THE IMPORTANCE OF AN EDUCATION

The purpose of going to college is to get an education. This declaration is so fundamental that you'd think we wouldn't need to say it. Yet many times students never realize their very reason for going to college. Some students never finish college, others get a degree but do not gain an education.

Getting an education is at the heart of why a person should go to college. Other good and useful things will accompany this experience. But the value and power of a good education is fundamental.

If, upon graduation, a student . . .

- has no desire to read a book
- has not developed the basic ability to think for himself or herself
- cannot articulate and argue for what he or she believes
- cannot write with clarity
- is not familiar with the most influential figures in history
- has little or no interest in current events
- has no sense of art and culture
- has little knowledge or appreciation for the natural world

. . . then the process, the school, and the student have all failed.

A college education should do at least three things for an individual.

First is *personal development.* College is designed to help you become a better person who is ready for the rigors of life. College is much more than "vocational training." For this reason, most schools have established a core curriculum—a set of courses every student must take, regardless of academic major.

This means everyone must take a certain amount of English, math, natural science, fine arts, social science, religion, and more. Academically, those requirements help push you into the deep. They will help you test the waters and test yourself. You will learn and grow and discover potential you may not know you have.

A liberal arts education strives to reflect the breadth of human culture through the study of the social sciences, the natural sciences, the arts, language, literature, and religion. The goal is to develop the whole person, which means the college quest is for wisdom as well as knowledge.

Second, besides personal development, a person's university training should provide the necessary *preparation for one's vocation.* The student who graduates with a degree in accounting should be prepared to sit for the Certified Public Accountant (CPA) exam. Nursing graduates, teacher education students, social work majors, and so on, should be ready to enter their chosen professions.

Third, a college education should make you a better person and prepare you for a meaningful vocation (or appropriate graduate program). But beyond those purposes, a college graduate should have developed *a philosophy of life* enabling him or her to live in community, foster wholesome and rewarding relationships, and embody a commitment to serve God and humanity.

You can do more than you think you can do academically, if you try. Don't be afraid to take some courses you think you may not like or will do less than your best in.

Isaac Newton, the scientist, said, "There are times when I seem to have been like a child playing on the seashore, finding now and then a prettier shell than ordinary, while all the time the great ocean of truth lay undiscovered before me."

You are going to college to learn, to get an education, to get ready for life. But that can't happen if you hug the shore, if you only play it safe, if you wade instead of swim, if you only splash about and play at going to college instead of diving in academically.

THE MARKS OF AN EDUCATED PERSON

He or she knows how to listen and hear. This is so simple, but in our distracted, busy world, one mark of an educated person is that he or she works hard to hear what others are saying. This means the person can track logical reasoning, follow an argument, hear the emotions behind the words.

An educated person can read and understand. This is simple to say but difficult to achieve. Skilled readers know how to read more than just the words. They read the ideas as well.

He or she can talk with nearly anyone. An educated person can communicate with a wide range of individuals. Educated people can carry on a solid conversation. They can give a speech or make a presentation.

Those who are truly educated can write clearly, concisely, and persuasively. An educated person can put words on paper. This one can express what is in his or her mind and heart so that others can understand and feel.

He or she can solve problems. This includes the ability to identify and analyze various components of a problem and the skill to determine an orderly solution.

An educated person appreciates intellectual reasoning and pursuit. This includes a love for learning and a deep appreciation for wisdom.

He or she practices respect and humility, tolerance and self-evaluation. To be educated means our mind is broadened to understand different points of view, while we realize our own limitations.

Educated people understand how to accomplish things. This represents the practical side of learning. To be educated is to be able to use your learning and skill for the good of others.

He or she nurtures and empowers others. When you're well educated, you understand that you are part of a community whose welfare is crucial to your own. In light of this, you reach out to help others.

BUILDING BLOCKS FOR ACADEMIC SUCCESS

Careful planning enhances academic success. If you want to finish the normal college course in four years, you will need to plan and monitor your schedule carefully.

Begin by getting organized. Find ways to study more effectively. This is hard because learning requires discipline and follow-through. But you can do it!

Take time to carefully read the college or university catalog. This booklet carefully describes degree programs, course descriptions, curricular options (international travel, internships, and so on), and academic majors and minors. An academic adviser will be assigned to help you. As soon as you determine your major, arrange for someone from that department to be your adviser, or at least consult a person from that area as you plan your schedule.

Remember, *you alone are responsible for your schedule.* If you have questions or don't understand requirements, talk to someone. You are not the first student to need advice. Asking for guidance is a smart step.

Don't assume "it'll all work out." Each year, some students come up short and can't graduate with their classmates because they have not met all of the academic requirements. That doesn't have to happen to you.

Often, students can "test out" of taking some required courses. Most colleges offer CLEP (College Level Examination Program) tests. You will be charged a slight fee for taking the exams, but testing out of courses can save both time and tuition. This also provides room in your schedule to take other courses of interest or to carry a lighter academic load and still graduate on time. Check with an admissions counselor early. These tests may have to be taken before classes begin and are often made available at orientation time.

Choosing a Major: Don't Rush

Choosing a major is important, but don't feel rushed and don't think your major in college will necessarily set the course for the rest of your life. It's merely a starting point. What's important is for you to follow your interests and discover what you love to do. If you are sure you want to be a doctor, then, yes, you need to settle that early enough to get the right premed courses. But even in those kinds of programs you will still have some latitude.

All of your friends may be rattling off majors/minors with such certainty. Don't be afraid to say, "Undecided." Here are some practical steps to help you as you think about choosing a major.

Consider which courses you've done well in previously and decide which major they have prepared you for.

Investigate the quality of the professors and courses. Ask your academic adviser which departments are well-regarded in their fields. Get a list of these departments' courses to see if they interest you. Also ask students who are majoring in these fields if they are satisfied with their programs and professors.

Do internships to get a feel for the kinds of jobs you could get with different majors.

Consider the requirements for any potential majors. Find out if they can be completed in four years or if they require graduate studies, and consider if you want to spend the necessary time and money.

What style of job or work intrigues you? Do you want to work with lots of people, or would you prefer to work alone? Do you want to be your own boss? Do you want to travel? Think about the different fields to which your major can be applied. Try to find a major that will offer flexibility when you are looking for a job.

Think about the growth of the field that interests you. Is the field expanding? Are graduates with your major being hired out of college, or do they need additional training?

Contemplate the earning potential and base salary of jobs related to certain majors. Think of the lifestyle you would like to maintain and how certain salaries may affect it.

Figure out what you love to do. Which fields of study spark your interest? Have you taken courses you particularly enjoyed?

Ask yourself if you have what it takes to succeed in your major.

Think about whether you would rather have a job you love with little pay, or have a job you can tolerate with substantial pay. Choose a career course accordingly.

Be flexible; you can change your major if you are unhappy with it.

You've Got Class!

While people can now take a course and even earn a degree on-line, most students find the heart of the academic program in the classroom experience.

GET READY

Once you have an overall academic plan—from reviewing the catalog and talking with your adviser—you must plan your class schedule for the semester. Each school publishes a course schedule. It will be up to you to choose your courses and plan your weekly schedule accordingly. Make sure the courses you take fulfill the requirements for your major and for the school's general education curriculum. If you're not sure, ask.

Some students seek to cluster their classes closely together, sometimes arranging to have class only in the mornings, or only on three or four days. This provides blocks of time for work, sports, or other activities.

Others, however, recognize the value in spreading the course work throughout the day and week. This enables students to have time before and after class to focus, prepare, follow up, and take a brief mental break before plunging into the next class.

Once you decide what courses you wish to take in a given semester, be sure to register (or preregister) as soon as possible. Most classes have a limited enrollment. *If you wait too late to register, the course you need at the time you need it may not be available!*

Also, remember that during your first year at college you should take a variety of courses to assess your abilities and interests. You may learn, even through an introductory course, that you don't want to pursue a given major after all. It's better to learn that early. The opposite is also true. You may find that you love and unexpectedly excel at a particular subject. This may shape your overall academic plan.

Consider these **Tips for Choosing Courses**.

Unless you are a strong student, **take a limited number of courses** the first semester. Getting off to a good start is *very important,* and a little lighter academic load could pay off in the long run. Of your first few courses, take one in the area of your prospective major. This will let you test the waters. The other courses should count for the general education requirements. This will provide some variety and will expose you to some areas of study that may hold particular interest for you.

As time goes by, **learn the value of taking only one or two "killer" courses per term.** You won't gain anything by loading yourself with heavy courses all at once. Often more than one "lab" class per semester is overdoing it because of all of the extra work involved.

Try to **vary the size and nature of the courses** you take each semester. This will add interest and variety to your academic routine.

Learn to **know the professors.** A great teacher can make all the difference for you. Ask around, you'll get lots of advice about who to take and who to avoid, if possible.

GET SET

Once your schedule is set, do a walk-through. Find the buildings, go to the rooms—know where you're headed and on which days and at what times. Also, get your books and materials ahead of time. If you can, learn in advance what to expect from the course and the professor. Each course and every teacher is different. Students as well as other faculty members can advise you.

Instructors generally provide a course syllabus on the first day of class. A syllabus is a guide to course requirements, which usually contains the following information:

• The course name, number, and meeting times. Make sure you are in the right class.

• Information about the instructor (name, office location, office hours, phone, E-mail).

• The textbook and other required or recommended readings. Textbooks change and are updated almost every year, so check for the correct edition of the text.

• Reading assignments with due dates.

• A list of written assignments, a description of the requirements for those assignments (style, length, grade value, due dates), and a description of other assignments that may be required.

• A schedule and description of tests and test dates.

• Policies concerning attendance and participation.

These items may be adjusted from time to time as the semester passes. If a change is announced, make sure you record the change. Often the syllabus is available online. You may wish to review that document for changes as the course unfolds.

Throughout the semester, you will find it pays to prepare for each class session ahead of time. (Actually, the professors expect this. Imagine that.)

• Complete the assignments.

• Do the assigned reading.

• Stay focused on when assignments are due.

Go

This is the starting line. Academic success begins in the classroom. You will not make any real progress toward your goal of getting through college if you fail to go to class—*regularly,* not occasionally. A set schedule and a daily and weekly routine will help you stay up with the progress of each class.

Why would students pay thousands of dollars for an education, then not go to class regularly? For some, it has to do with that newfound freedom you get when you first go to college. Occasionally, that freedom translates into a "What can I get away with today?" attitude. Cutting class may give you a sense of power, of being able to do whatever you feel like. But you can pay a substantial price for such an exercise in freedom. Do you want to really feel free and powerful? Start knocking down good grades in tough classes—that is a terrific feeling, and it begins by showing up for class! Freedom means responsibility.

WHAT TO DO IN CLASS

Choose the right seat. Often you can be more involved in classroom activities and can pay closer attention if you sit near the front, away from as many distractions (windows, doors, or classmates) as possible. The front seats are the power seats.

Obviously, not everyone can sit in the front row, and occasionally, professors will use assigned seating. Wherever you sit, make sure you are as comfortable as possible and that you can see and participate fully in class activities.

Become an active listener. Many people have a harder time remembering what they hear than what they read. We acquire 83 percent of our information from seeing and only 11 percent from hearing. And we remember only 20 percent of what we hear, compared to 30 percent of what we see and 50 percent when we both hear and see.

Most of our forgetting occurs almost immediately. Researchers tested one group of students on how much they could remember from a lecture and found that within 24 hours, most had forgotten more than half.[1] It is a

---

1. Robert Holkeboer and Laurie Walker, *Right from the Start,* 3rd ed. (Belmont, Calif.: Wadsworth Publishing Company, 1999), 95.

paradox that listening is both the easiest path to learning and one of the hardest skills to master.

As you become a better listener, you will be a more successful student and a more popular person. Don't forget that . . .

becoming a better listener
means better retention
which means better learning
which means better grades.

A significant difference lies between hearing and listening. The ears hear when sound waves vibrate against the eardrum. Hearing is physiological—a bodily function. Listening, on the other hand, is a deliberate activity of the brain that seeks to interpret and store those sounds. If your brain is not listening to what your ears hear, you will rapidly forget what you heard (or more accurately, what you didn't hear in the first place).

The skill of listening requires mindful involvement. In the classroom or study environment, your mind must be fully engaged in listening for key words and important ideas. Listening includes asking questions, in your mind, as you seek to understand what is being said.

Active listening gives you a tremendous advantage over passive hearing, because human beings can think at least four times faster than we can speak. This means you will have at least three-quarters of every class period to process what the speaker says into a coherent set of notes, think about and evaluate what is said, and relate it to your experience and learning.[2]

Be a participant, not a spectator. Participate in the discussion or the demonstrations. Ask questions. Show interest.

---

2. Ibid.

Take notes carefully and consistently. Note-taking helps you grasp the material as it is presented and also provides you with an important resource for review and test preparation.

Too often students take notes passively rather than actively. They confuse note-taking with taking dictation, trying to write down everything they hear. That approach is nearly impossible. It is an ineffective way to capture the important parts of a lecture or classroom presentation. Remember when it comes to taking notes, you are a student, not just a stenographer.

Listen for and record key ideas. Usually, by taking short, concise notes, you will have the key information you need to review. And again, if you have read or even just looked over the assigned material before class, you will be much more aware of important points from the lecture.

Avoid complete sentences. You don't need to write your notes in complete, grammatically correct sentences. You will lose valuable time with full sentences.

Develop an outline. An outline helps you organize and note the relationship of the various points of the lecture.

Don't leave out any fundamental ideas. Don't tell yourself, "I'll remember that." Write it down.

Review your notes after class. When class is over, take a few minutes to review and make sure your notes are complete.

WHAT TO DO AFTER CLASS

Clarify any questions regarding material presented or assignments made with the professor or with other students *before you leave the classroom*. Be sure you have a clear understanding of what you should do to prepare for the next class session.

Find a place to review and organize your notes. Take a few moments for a brief review as soon as you can after the class. This can increase your long-term retention of the material by as much as 50 percent.

Also, a quick review will help you as you schedule your study time later. It will also highlight materials you may need to assemble from the library or the Internet. It may even reveal if you missed something and need to find a classmate who can fill in the blanks.

Complete all assignments. You simply cannot expect to pass a college course if you don't complete the assignments on time or do them right. Take pride in your work. How you do the assignments shows you are not just going through the motions of going to class but are taking your work seriously. For example, an essay that has been carefully proofread and neatly typed shows you have put work into it and care about its appearance.

IF YOU HAVE TO MISS A CLASS

Contact the professor *before* if possible, after for sure.

Find someone who was in class and get notes.

Know the options and consequences of dropping/ withdrawing from a course.

LEARNING TO LEARN

Only a fraction of your actual learning will occur inside the classroom. Learning to learn successfully takes a lot of hard work.

DEVELOPING SOLID STUDY HABITS

The key to any good study routine is based on two simple concepts—organization and consistency. No matter what study methods you use, you will learn more, retain it longer, and perform better on tests if you approach studying in an organized and consistent manner.

When you have developed or adopted a system that works for you, you will only have one thing left to do: stick to it! Make sure you study in generally the same way every time. Soon your study routines will become a habit, studying will become second nature, and the organization and consistency required to study effectively will happen almost automatically.

Set a study schedule. One key to successful study is to establish a study schedule and follow that schedule consistently. Designated study times should carry the same weight in your planning as work and class schedules. Focus on the fact that study time is the pathway to success. If you don't study, you can't pass the exams or complete the assignments. If you can't pass the exams or complete the assignments, you won't pass the course. If you don't pass your courses, you can't stay in school. If you don't stay in school, you'll never graduate. If you

don't graduate, you can't reap the social, economic, and
personal benefits of a college education. Learning to
study is not an option.

Create the right study environment. Creating the
right environment for study involves more than just
where you study. It also includes consideration of *when*
you should study and *how* you should study.

Ideally you should do most of your studying in one
place. This should be a comfortable place, free from interruptions, well lit, and where you have access to the study
aids (computer, resource materials, and so on) you may
need. In addition to this regular place for study, you may
need to do some additional study and preparation in the
library, the lab, the practice studio, or with a study group.

Give your best time to the most important things. Are
you most productive and alert in the morning, the after-
noon, early evening, or late at night? Your studying will
take less time and be more effective if you do it when you
are most alert.

WHAT ABOUT STUDY GROUPS?

Many students benefit from studying regularly with a
small group of others. Such a group provides accountability to help ensure that assignments are completed and
that test preparation stays on schedule. These groups are
voluntary, self-formed, and meet regularly. Their purpose
is to help students review, study, and prepare for tests.

Study groups should be small—three or four students.
Group members need to be students you respect, who are
serious about learning, and who are responsible to meet
the requirements of the group. The group should meet in
a place appropriate for study with a leader to help the
group stay on task. Without proper leadership, groups
can easily drift into socialization.

Although study groups are helpful, you will still need

some private study time to review the material alone. Your classmates can help you learn, but they cannot learn for you.

How Do You Learn Best?

Learning increases with the level of your interest. You can develop an interest in subjects you don't expect to like if you will be open-minded and gain a basic understanding of the subject.

We become more interested in subjects that are defined in terms of real experience and concrete problems that affect our lives. If you have trouble getting interested in a subject, look for ways that subject impacts your life. You will learn more as you connect the lectures and reading with your own life.

We are also most likely to learn when we write and speak about a given subject. When we write something or repeat a word or phrase out loud, we are more apt to remember it.

Learning is also often enhanced when we learn with others. Most lasting learning takes place in a social context. That is why class attendance and participation are so important.

How do you learn? Think about what you do when you have to learn something new. You probably approach the task in a similar way each time. This means that over time you have developed a pattern of behavior that you use (almost instinctively) for new learning. This pattern is called a learning style. Understanding your style may help you increase your ability to learn.

Some people learn through concrete experiences such as feeling, touching, seeing, and hearing. Others best learn using mental or visual conceptualization.

After receiving information, a person needs to process it. This can happen either by experimentation (doing something with the information) or by thinking.

These variables are expressed in various learning dimensions:

- **Concrete experience**—learning from specific experiences
- **Reflective observation**—careful observation, looking for the meaning of things, reading, and trying to view ideas, thoughts, and information from different perspectives
- **Abstract conceptualization**—logical analysis of ideas, questioning, comparing, and contrasting
- **Active experimentation**—trying out new ideas and information

Most students are one of the following types of learners. As you think about going to college, *you need to have a sense of how you best learn.* Which of the following styles best describes you?

- **Type I Learner:** You are a "passive" learner. You accept other people's analyses and opinions without necessarily questioning what is being presented.
- **Type II Learner:** You want to look at things from different points of view. You would rather watch and think than take action. You like using your imagination to solve problems.
- **Type III Learner:** You like solving problems and finding practical solutions and uses for what you are learning. You prefer technical tasks and clear answers.
- **Type IV Learner:** You are concise and logical. Abstract ideas and concepts are more important to you than people issues. Practicality is less important to you than a logical explanation.

It may also be helpful for you to understand the difference between deductive reasoning and inductive reasoning.

Deductive reasoning is a process where conclusions flow from the general to the particular. When learning, this means you prefer to look at the big picture first, then get the details. For example, when learning a new game, you want to know the rules and clearly understand the object of the game before you start to play. If this is your primary way of thinking but you get only details without being given an overall concept, you may be confused by not knowing how all of this information fits together.

Inductive reasoning is a process that starts with particulars and moves toward generalizations. In a learning setting, you would like to see some examples when first learning a new subject, before developing an overview. When learning a new game, you are content to learn the rules as you go along.

A person uses both types of reasoning, but generally prefers one or the other. Knowing which you prefer will help you process and organize material for learning.

Recognize there are various levels of learning:

Information. The first level of learning is to acquire basic facts. However, a person can know facts and figures without really understanding their significance.

Recognition. The ability to recall or recognize information at a later time than when you first learned the information.

Comprehension. The ability to grasp the meaning of what is being communicated, and to use the idea or information by relating it to other ideas or materials.

Application. The ability to use ideas, principles, or theories in particular specific situations.

Analysis. The ability to break down a communication into constituent parts to understand the whole. This includes identifying various parts, understanding the relationship between parts, and recognizing the organization principles involved.

Synthesis. The ability to put together parts and elements into a unified organization or whole. It is the ability to see and understand the relationship between items.

Evaluation. The ability to judge the value of ideas, procedures, and methods using the right criteria.

Don't be satisfied with just gathering data, lists, or

recognizing information. To learn, you must practice these procedures.

The Library Is More than a Place for Miniature Golf

One favorite winter activity each year at a Midwestern college is a miniature golf tournament held on a makeshift course laid out in the library. It is great fun and helps remove stuffy ideas often associated with libraries. However, this kind of fun is a brief substitute for the other kinds of fun you can find in a library/resource learning center.

If you want to succeed academically, you will need to become familiar with the library and the learning technologies available on most campuses. You'll discover the joy of finding how much help is actually available to you as you prepare your assignments and study for exams. Some students, at least at first, seem to think of the library as a big warehouse for books—but libraries offer much more.

At your fingertips—besides books, libraries offer:
- Reference material: encyclopedias, indexes, dictionaries, almanacs, bibliographies
- Electronically stored materials including a wide range of computer-accessed resources
- Newspapers and magazines
- Maps and atlases
- Academic journals
- Interlibrary loan services
- Video and audio recordings
- Copy machines and services
- Computer labs
- Quiet study areas

These facilities and the people who staff them have one purpose—to help you succeed academically. Most schools provide a library orientation. Every student should become familiar with the library, the various learning technologies available, and the library staff.

Librarians are the most vital resource in the library. They are not "book police" but are there to answer questions and guide you toward the resources you need. This can save you hours of frustration and distraction. Don't be shy or afraid to ask for help—that's a sign of intelligence, not ignorance.

DEVELOP YOUR READING SKILLS

The reading of all good books is like conversation with the finest men of past centuries.[3] Reading is fundamental. The better you learn to read, the better you will do in college. Reading, like most activities, can be improved with practice.

The most common problems students face when reading for classes isn't tough vocabulary or work overload, it's the way their minds seem to wander, finding interest in everything other than the assignment.

Good readers read for purpose.

Poor readers read aimlessly.

Good readers read critically, thinking as they go.

Poor readers accept what they read without processing it.

Good readers assimilate thoughts and ideas.

Poor readers get lost in the muddle of words and sentences.

Good readers understand its importance and value.

Poor readers see it as a chore to be endured.

Even if you are not a great reader, you can still succeed if you will be sure to actually read your assignments and take notes on what you have read.

---

3. Descartes as quoted by Ron Fry in *Improve Your Reading,* 4th ed. (Franklin Lakes, N.J.: Career Press, 2000), 113.

One important tip is to read ahead, rather than behind, your professors' class presentations. Reading ahead takes no more time, yet it greatly impacts your learning. If you will read ahead in the textbook, when your professor is lecturing you will already know part of what he or she is covering.

Reading Tips

First, **look over the chapter** or section so you will have some idea what material is being covered.

Look for headings, subheadings, highlighted terms and summaries.

Read each section thoroughly. Read quickly, but concentrate on comprehension, not speed.

Take notes immediately after you finish a section. You may wish to construct a brief outline of what was presented.

With a highlighter, **mark the key points** as you read or when you review your notes.

To Increase Your Reading Speed

- Focus your attention and concentration.
- Eliminate distractions.
- Choose a comfortable environment.
- Don't get sidetracked on a single word or sentence you don't understand at first.
- Try to grasp sentences rather than words.
- Don't read aloud or even silently say the words.
- Practice!

To Comprehend Better What You Read

- Read for ideas and concepts, paying close attention to the first sentence of each paragraph.
- Review and rethink as you go along. Test yourself to see if you are understanding what you are reading.
- Don't be hesitant to reread if you are not getting it.
- Summarize what you have read. Be able to put it in your own words.

What you retain depends on what you understand. It has little to do with how fast you read, how much you highlight, or how well you outline. Comprehension rests on your ability to gather the facts, grasp the main idea, note the sequence, and draw conclusions. Not everything you read will require you to comprehend on all four levels. But you will need to touch on each as you go along.

How to Skim a Text

You don't need to read every word of a given book or article to determine if that resource will be helpful to you. If you can skim a text effectively, you will be able to use your time more efficiently. Here are some tips:

- Read introductions, conclusions, and summary paragraphs.

Textbooks: Cutting the Cost

One surprise at college is the cost of textbooks. Students spend up to several hundred dollars per semester for books. There are, however, a few ways to help cut the cost.

- **Buy used textbooks.** Your school bookstore usually sells used copies of textbooks. The downside is that used books have often been marked up by the previous owner. Bookstores also generally don't have enough used books to meet the demand for them. So, go early.

You may also want to get a class list or at ask around about the courses you will take next. If you know people in the class, or students who previously took the course, you may want to ask one of them about buying the book directly from him or her.

- **Use the Internet.** Check out used book services for used books or for new books at a lower price.
- **Use a library copy.** Others may have this thought in mind, so the book may not always be available when you need it. Sometimes the professor requests that a copy be placed "on reserve," which means you may read it in the library but may not check it out.
- **Share books.** Some students who are friends or roommates and have the same class buy the textbook together and share it. This method does have some problems, but it can work and will save you some money.
- **Sell your own books** when you have finished using them. When you buy a book, ask if the store has a buyback policy.

- Read the first and last lines of paragraphs.
- Look at illustrations, graphs, and charts.
- Read the words and phrases set in boldface or italics.
- Note the sections you may wish to reread more carefully.

ROADBLOCKS TO LEARNING

Some students are hindered in their academic pursuit by certain roadblocks. Can you identify which of these areas might give you trouble?

- Lack of organization
- No clear academic goals
- No plan of attack
- Perfectionism
- Procrastination
- Interruptions
- Learning disabilities
- Lack of discipline
- Too much social life
- Sports
- TV or recreational Internet use

You can overcome all of these by early detection and a will to succeed. Don't let these things rob you of the education you are seeking.

PRESENTING WHAT YOU'VE LEARNED

After you have learned information, you still have a bit to go toward getting a good grade. Part of making a good grade is not only learning the information but also being able to present the information in a manner that lets your professors know you've truly learned.

LEARN TO WRITE RIGHT

One difference you will probably encounter between your classes in high school and your college courses is that you will be required to write more in college. Most courses will require some type of term paper. Don't just start writing—plan first.

If you just start writing, you will often end up with a jumbled set of sentences and a disjointed set of facts and observations. Writing is communication. The quality and flow of your ideas is the most important element of your writing. You can enhance your presentation of those ideas if you follow these:

Steps in Writing a Term Paper

The purposes of a term paper are to impart information and develop thought. For each written assignment you will need to:

Start early. Not having enough time will undermine the process and result in a poor product.

Choose a subject. Sometimes the subject is assigned, at other times you must choose a topic. If you have any doubts about the suitability of your subject, talk to your professor.

Develop a list of questions and subtopics so you will know what you are looking for as you gather material.

Do the necessary reading and research. This process will drive the content of the paper as you gather facts and key ideas.

Make an outline that can guide you as you organize your material and write the essay.

Write a first draft. Begin with a brief introduction that states the purpose and describes the process you will follow in the paper. Then, follow your outline, developing your thoughts as you go.

Leave it for a while and then **reread** it, making corrections and improvements as you go.

Prepare a final draft to submit to the professor.

Always keep a copy for yourself. If your paper disappears (that does happen!), you will have a backup copy.

Term papers should be accurate, interesting, mechanically and grammatically correct, and neatly presented.

How to Write a College Paper *(in 25 questionable steps)*

1. Sit in a straight, comfortable chair in a well-lighted place with plenty of freshly sharpened pencils.

2. Read the assignment carefully, to make certain you understand it.

3. Walk to the vending machines and buy a Mountain Dew to help you concentrate.

4. Stop at the third floor on the way back and visit with your friend from class. If your friend hasn't started the paper yet either, you can both walk to McDonald's and buy a hamburger to help you concentrate.

5. When you get back to your room, sit in a straight, comfortable chair in a clean, well-lighted place with plenty of freshly sharpened pencils.

6. Read the assignment again to be absolutely sure you understand it.

7. You know, you haven't written to that kid you met at camp in the fourth grade.

8. Go look at your teeth in the bathroom mirror.

9. Rearrange your CDs in alphabetical order.

10. Listen to a favorite CD and that's it—I mean it. As soon as the CD is over, you are going to start that paper.

11. Phone your friend on the third floor and ask if he's started writing yet. Exchange derogatory remarks about your professor, the university, and the world at large.

12. Sit in a straight, comfortable chair in a clean, well-lighted place with plenty of freshly sharpened pencils.

13. Read the assignment again; roll the words across your tongue; savor their special sound.

14. Check the newspaper listings to make sure you aren't missing something truly worthwhile on TV.

15. Phone your friend on the third floor to see if he is watching TV. Discuss the finer points of the plot.

16. Go look at your tongue in the bathroom mirror.

17. Organize your pens and paper clips.

18. Look through your roommate's book of pictures from home. Ask who everyone is.

19. Sit down and think seriously about your plans for the future.

20. Open your door to see if anything is happening in the hall.

21. Sit in a straight, comfortable chair in a clean, well-lighted place with plenty of freshly sharpened pencils.

22. Read the assignment one more time.

23. Scoot your chair across the room to the window and watch the sunrise.

24. Lie facedown on the floor and moan.

25. Get up and sit in a straight, comfortable chair in a clean, well-lighted place with plenty of freshly sharpened pencils.

Get it? Writing a paper is not easy, but *the hardest part is getting started.* So, start early, gather your resources, and begin.

TESTING

Tests give us feedback and help us know if we are making appropriate progress. A natural anxiety accompanies this process, but taking tests doesn't have to be an overwhelming experience if you will note the following tips.

General Tips for Test-Taking

Put your name on your test.

Read the directions. If you are not sure what they mean, don't be afraid to ask the instructor.

Listen carefully to any instructions given with the test.

Scan the test before you start. Note ideas that come to mind and budget your time.

Don't panic. Begin by answering the questions you do know. Often, as you think about the tough questions, ideas gradually come to you.

Be sure to write something. Don't leave questions blank if you can help it. It's better to get some credit than none at all.

Focus on the test—don't let your mind wander, don't get distracted.

Use the allotted time—don't see how fast you can finish.

Don't let students leaving early distract or discourage you.

On **matching tests** with multiple answers, do the questions you know first. One answer you do know may give you clues to other answers you may not know at first.

On **fill-in-the-blank tests,** look for clues in the sentence structure or other words used.

On **multiple-choice tests**—after you have read a question, look away and consider the answer before looking at the responses. Then read all of the answers carefully, eliminating answers to help find the correct one.

When taking an ***essay test,*** read the question carefully. Take note of key words such as *compare, contrast, list, give an example, summarize, trace,* and so on. These words will give you both a starting point and some insight into the instructor's expectations.

Start with a thesis and an outline, use transitions and key phrases, be concise but as thorough as possible in the time allotted.

Write legibly.

When you are finished, look back over the test to make sure you completed it all and that you are satisfied with your answers.

After the test is graded and returned to you, review it. You will not only learn from your mistakes but also improve your test-taking ability. Both of these will help you on the next exam.

Work daily (last-minute cramming will not make up for poor preparation).

Over time, try to learn the testing style and habits of various professors. You should be able to recognize what each teacher believes is important and be better prepared for tests.

Ask ahead of time what kind of test to expect: essay, fill-in-the-blank, and so on.

Your performance on tests will improve and your test anxiety will diminish if you are listening actively, taking consistent notes, and reviewing carefully.

A WORD ABOUT FACULTY

Not all professors are created equal. It is a little tough your first semester to know which teachers are best for you, but as you plan your next semester, you should be able to learn which professors you might prefer.

It is helpful if you will get to know (and get to know about) the faculty. Consider these ways to find the best professors:

- Ask other students—they know!
- Ask your adviser for advice.
- Note any professor who gets an award for teaching or is recognized as faculty member of the year.
- Ask for a copy of a course syllabus so you can assess what the teacher expects in a given class.
- Talk with a prospective professor. Make an appointment or just drop by to ask, "Would you tell me a little about this course you are teaching next semester?" His or her answer and the way you are treated will tell you about both the course and the teacher.
- Some students, if they are unsure about what to take in a given semester, will overenroll. They sign up for more courses than they intend to take, and after a week or so, they drop the one or two courses they least like.

Your professors will enrich your life, challenge you to think and grow, and mentor you in many ways beyond class. If you are attending a relatively small college, you should be able to get acquainted with several of your major professors. It is not uncommon for students to be invited to a professor's home or to eat with a professor in the college dining room. You will also have opportunities to talk with professors at university events.

Don't forget that nearly all college professors are genuinely interested in students. Don't be shy about taking the initiative to get to know your professors outside of class.

Remember, regardless of the professor, you can learn and make the grade you want. Learning depends on the student as well as the instructor. Your college's academic expectations are spelled out in the college catalog. Although these requirements vary from one school to another, generally you, as a student, are responsible to attend class regularly, complete the assignments on time, and participate in required class activities.

If a serious illness or necessary absence prevents you from completing the course, you may, at the professor's discretion, be given an Incomplete (I) grade. You will then have a designated time period—from a few weeks to a full year—to finish the course work. If you complete the work within the time allotted, the (I) will be changed to a regular letter grade. If you fail to complete the work, the Incomplete is then converted to a failing grade.

Generally if your GPA falls below 2.00 (C average) you are automatically placed on academic probation, during which time you may be restricted from certain campus activities such as intercollegiate sports.

What a Professor Expects of You

- To attend class
- To pay attention
- To be interested
- To participate
- To communicate, ask questions
- To do the assignments
- To be respectful and courteous
- Doughnuts once in a while

GPA (Grade Point Average)

Your grade point average is the standard measure of academic accomplishment. It is a clear barometer of how well you are doing. If you have a strong GPA, you might receive more scholarship dollars, more freedom in planning your courses, and access to special programs and opportunities. Later, this will be one of the indicators employers or graduate schools consider.

While having a strong GPA is no guarantee you will get into the grad school you want or land the job you desire, a weak GPA can knock you out of the running from the start. Therefore, focusing on having the highest GPA you can possibly earn should be a top priority.

A common myth about GPA is that it measures intelligence. That is only part of the story. What the GPA really measures is a student's determination, commitment, dedication to success, and willingness to work hard. It is hard to raise a GPA, so make your first semester count.

MORE ACADEMIC NOTES TO REMEMBER

ACADEMIC INTEGRITY/CHEATING

Integrity is important in all of life. Cheating in your academic life will sow seeds of destruction because once you decide to cheat, it becomes a pattern and spreads to other areas of your life. Cheating can bring very serious consequences. To cheat in business is to open yourself to lawsuits, fines, loss of credentials, and public embarrassment.

Academic cheating most often takes the form of cheating on tests or plagiarism (using someone else's work as your own). Be proactive from the start of your college career to establish a pattern of academic honesty. If you have cheated in the past, break the pattern, begin again, and get a fresh start.

If You Have Academic Trouble

Many students hit an academic roadblock somewhere along the way toward a college degree. Not every student is gifted in every area of study. Math students may struggle with literature. Art students may not naturally excel in biology. You can still finish strong academically if you will follow these tips:

Face the problem immediately. Almost any academic

problem can be overcome if you don't ignore it. Remember, problems don't solve themselves. Be proactive.

If you find a class session or assignment difficult, **review the basics:** Did you read the material before class? Did you complete your previous assignments? Did you read the directions carefully? If not, circle back and catch up right away.

Before the next class session, **contact the professor or teaching assistant.** He or she will be glad that you want to get it right.

If problems continue, **find a tutor.** You may be able to simply get help from a friend in class. If that is not possible, ask the professor, the departmental secretary, or the learning resource center for a suggestion in finding a paid tutor. This could be money well spent. It will be cheaper than retaking a course or losing a scholarship.

If nothing seems to work and it will simply take too much effort to survive, **you may wish to drop the class.** If you do decide to drop a course, follow the procedure to "officially" drop the course—don't just quit going to class!

If this pattern is repeated, you may need to consider changing majors.

International Study: Growing Abroad

Almost every college and university in America provides some opportunity for international travel and study. Often, this is a requirement for you to complete certain majors (languages, international business, and others). Your freshman year is the time to start thinking about and planning for an international study opportunity.

After you are settled in the routine of your first semester, ask around. Find out what programs are available and which professors coordinate the various study programs. You will need to plan your schedule carefully to get the necessary courses you will need to graduate and still have time to take a semester for foreign study.

Also, you can expect to pay more for the semester you spend away from campus. There are often travel expenses and miscellaneous fees besides tuition and room and board. If you plan early enough, you can spread the financial impact of such a program beyond a single semester.

Not only is taking college courses in another country a stretching and enriching experience, but what you learn outside of the classroom will be an education as well.

PROCRASTINATION: READ THIS LATER IF YOU WISH

Procrastination is a habit, not a fatal flaw. It takes persistence to change, but *you can do it*. Here's how:

Clarify Your Personal Goals

1. Articulate and write down your personal goals. Post them on your door, mirror, notebook, anywhere you'll see them frequently.

2. Be sure the task you think you should do is really important to you and leads to your goal. If your actions aren't in line with your intentions, perhaps you should change your intentions: "I said I'd study history now, but it's more important to rest after my test today. I'll plan to do it tomorrow morning."

Manage Your Time Effectively

1. If you don't know how to manage your time, learn. Break your goal into little parts. List the steps you must take to accomplish your goal. Write a plan for yourself. Make a schedule. Establish a regular time each day to work toward your goal. Get out of a disorganized lifestyle and make working toward your goal part of your routine.

2. Organize your environment. Gather the tools and supplies you'll need. Make sure your place of study is well-lighted and comfortable. It is difficult to organize

your thoughts and be productive in a chaotic environment.

3. If you aren't sure how to reach your goal, learn. For example, if you aren't clear about an assignment, consult with your professor. Build this appointment into your schedule.

4. Start early.

5. Start small and easily. Build gradually.

Change Your Attitude

1. Do you feel that the world is too difficult? that you are inadequate to meet its challenges? that you cannot function without a lot of approval? Are you frustrated with others' limitations? Do you expect perfection from yourself and others? Are you convinced that disaster hinges on your actions? These are immobilizing, self-defeating attitudes and beliefs.

2. Remind yourself of the emotional and physical consequences of procrastination. Then remind yourself of the value and benefits of not procrastinating.

3. Concentrate on little bits and pieces of your project; don't think "all or nothing."

4. Know your escapes and avoidances: self-indulgence? socializing? reading? doing it yourself? overdoing it? running away? daydreaming? Call yourself on those things.

Change Your Behavior

1. Use your friends. Set up a contract with someone to get something done. Make an appointment to study with a friend who has no difficulty studying. Consult with someone who can help you with your task. Meet with a friend for support, someone who'll listen and who'll share your highs and lows.

2. Make something you normally enjoy contingent upon doing the avoided task: "I'll work on my term paper in the library half an hour before going to play racquetball."

3. Keep your tasks visibly in front of you: set up reminders, signs, slogans, notes, lists.

4. Use your impulsiveness. When you get going, keep going. Do something when you think of it—don't just think about it. Do instant, tiny things.

5. Do something daily. Agree to start a project and stay with it for five minutes. Consider another five minutes at the end of the first.

6. Establish priorities among tasks according to the degree of unpleasantness. Start with the most unpleasant task and work down until you get to the easier ones.

7. If you've got something hard to do, rehearse it in your imagination or with someone. Work the bugs out; don't terrify yourself.

8. Be sure the rest of your life is in good shape . . . so your awful task is less awful within the context of a good general quality of life.

9. Get enough sleep. Contrary to popular opinion, you cannot catch up on the weekend. You can get rested on a weekend, but you cannot go back and sleep for the time you lost earlier in the week. It's like skipping lunch on Tuesday and then eating two lunches on Saturday. That does not make up for the energy and nutrition you needed but did not have on Tuesday.

Accept Yourself

1. Give yourself time to change.
2. Expect and forgive backsliding.
3. Give yourself credit for anything you do.
4. Forgive yourself when you fail.
5. Move on!

Part 4

THE SOCIAL ADVENTURE

Harvard cost me too much for what it taught me; but it charged me nothing for the most valuable thing I got there, my friends.
—Henry David Thoreau

A Whole New World of People

One of the best parts of your college life is the opportunity to
- Meet new people
- Learn to value differences
- Develop an appreciation for diversity

As you get started in the college environment, take advantage of a fresh start socially. What an adventure! Don't hang out with the same crowd all the time. Go out and meet new people. Learn what it takes to get along, to live in community, to give and take.

Push yourself to try some new things. Get involved in a student organization. Find a place to make a difference, to contribute to the university. Take a risk now and then—don't be afraid to fail.

As humans, we derive our sense of identity, in part, by comparing ourselves with others. If no one ever asks you a question or challenges you, if no one ever seeks to bring out of you some hidden thought or reenforces your ideals or values, you will not discover who you are.

And when another person asks for help, you discover certain dimensions of compassion you didn't know about before. When someone attempts to influence you to do what is not good, you discover a level of courage and commitment you might not ever have known before.

Friends and classmates provide necessary feedback, both formally and informally. They help you know how you are doing in life. Students who live and go to school together help each other grow and learn.

MAKING FRIENDS

The friends you make in college could influence your life for a long time. Be friendly and respect everyone, but carefully choose those close friends who will most influence your college experience. They need to be the kind of friends who will bring out the best in you and who demonstrate a genuine interest in knowing you. You will need friends to listen and share in your good times, as well as those who will listen to your problems and accept you when you are not at your best.

Friendships don't just happen automatically. You make them happen by reaching out to others, by being a friend. Here are some important steps to finding friends once you get to campus.

Be available. Get out of your dorm room and mix with others. Make eye contact, speak to those around you, introduce yourself, ask someone a question. Don't be obnoxious and don't be a pest, but reach out in natural ways. *Remember that no matter how self-assured someone else may seem at first, nearly everyone is in the same situation—on a campus without many friends.*

Sometimes when you reach out to a person, he or she might not return the gesture. Don't let that shake you. It doesn't mean anything is wrong with you or with that person. It is just a natural part of socialization.

Develop different avenues. Some students will become friends in the dorm, where you see them regularly. Other friendships may develop through class assignments. Sometimes you will find a friend at work, on a sports team, or in a club: Let the natural web of activities become an avenue for you to develop different kinds of friendships.

Be a good listener. Listening is a wonderful social tool to building a bridge of friendship. As you listen to others, you demonstrate your value for who they are and what they have to say. Sometimes you will consciously need to resist the temptation to talk about yourself, so you can listen to some else. If that person wants to be a friend, he or she will soon give you a chance to talk. If conversation lags, ask an open-ended question, "How do you feel about . . . ?"

Be the kind of person others want to have as a friend. Are you the kind of person others want to be around? Are you fun to be with? Are you trustworthy and thoughtful? Take pride in your appearance and be positive in your outlook and attitude.

Don't take your friends for granted. Once a friendship begins to develop, continue to nurture it. Keep your commitments. Don't be possessive of your friends' time. Be honest, return favors, and be patient. Don't borrow without asking. Never compromise a confidential conversation.

CULTURE SHOCK

Culture is defined by the ways a group of people define themselves—clothing, diet, traditions, language, music, and so on. Every college campus has a certain culture as well as subcultures. When you first arrive on campus, you might not know exactly what to expect. This could result in a brief period of culture shock.

Culture shock is a state of bewilderment and distress experienced by an individual who is exposed to a new culture. When a person moves into new surroundings without familiar landmarks, but with different faces and a different pace of life, he or she feels a certain level of uneasiness. This shock often causes homesickness. It is natural to want to go home where it's safe, familiar, and comfortable. *Stick it out*—this will pass.

Most students will probably experience some level of culture shock during the first semester of college life. They may feel like the scarecrow in *The Wizard of Oz* who said, "Part of me is over here and part of me is over there!"

But this is natural and doesn't need to last very long. While you cannot avoid culture shock, you can minimize it by recognizing its presence and reaching out to others who may feel the same way. When school gets underway and your routine is established, the new patterns will become familiar and comfortable.

DIVERSITY

To be prejudiced is to "prejudge" an individual based on some social indicator such as race, gender, appearance, handicap, or religion. In reality, all of us carry a certain level of prejudice. To admit our predispositions is a first step to overcoming them.

One mark of an educated individual is an ability to tolerate and accept other opinions and other people. American culture, by its nature, is a melting pot of individuals from various backgrounds around the world. This diversity is both a challenge and a wonderful opportunity. It calls for more sensitivity than if everyone were from the same background, but it also provides a richness of social interchange.

The basic rule in dealing with people of different races, regions, accents, genders, or religious faith is respect. Give it and you will get it.

Most people want to fit in and be accepted, but you don't have to change who you are to do so. Take your time, watch, listen, and learn, then you will naturally begin to adjust to the social environment of the campus.

DIVING INTO DORM LIFE

A college residence hall provides a good transitional environment from home to living on your own. It offers structure, support, and security while giving you a lot of personal freedom.

A residence hall is also a great place to make new friends and develop personally as you learn how to live in community. This is especially true your freshman year. It's fun to live with people who are all in the same boat as you—getting adjusted and trying to make friends.

Most dormitories are near the heart of campus, which is convenient (especially if you go to school in a cold climate). Living in a residence hall also makes it easier to get involved in campus activities—they are just steps away. Plus, something is usually going on in the dorm itself—a bull session, a study group, television, lots of music, and conversation.

ROOMMATES

For some students, college roommates become lifelong friends; for others, a roommate becomes one of the biggest problems they face in school. Generally, you can expect something somewhere in between those two extremes.

Roommates don't have to become best friends. They don't have to go everywhere and do everything together—but roommates do have to live together, and that takes special commitments such as respect, courtesy, communication, and the ability to resolve conflicts.

If you want your experience with your roommate to be positive, decide together that you both have the right, obligation, and freedom to establish open lines of communication. If you find out ahead of time who your roommate will be, call that person and introduce yourself. Start planning before you move in how you might like to furnish your room (no need for both of you to bring a refrigerator).

Talk about how you can best respect each other's privacy and individual space. Give your roommate a copy of your class and work schedule. He or she will know when to expect you and where to find you if necessary.

Work together to establish a regular schedule that will make time for study, relaxation (TV/music, visitors from down the hall), and sleeping. If each roommate tries these things at different times, it won't be pretty. Also, make time to clean regularly.

One more tip: If you plan to share a dorm room with a high school pal, you might want to consider living in the same dorm but having two different rooms. This way you can stay friendly, but you also have the opportunity to meet new people. If you're always hanging around with a friend from high school, it might be harder for others to get to know you.

Don't worry too much about all of this—rarely will your worst fears come true. In fact, you could be on the verge of meeting your new best friend.

TOP TEN WAYS TO
MAKE YOUR ROOMMATE HAPPY[4]

10. Buy your own shampoo, soap, and deodorant—and use them.

---

4. Taken in part from Suzette Tyler, *Been There (Should've) Done That* (Haslett, Mich.: Front Porch Press, 1997), 37.

9. Wash your cereal bowl and socks before they're green and fuzzy.

8. Keep your wet towel off the beds.

7. Don't have too many overnight visits from friends from home.

6. Don't hit the "snooze" button a thousand times for an eight o'clock class you're not going to anyway.

5. Keep your beverages off the computer.

4. Don't take a call and then announce, "Someone called, but I don't remember who . . ." Write it down.

3. Don't disappear when it's time to pay for the pizza.

2. Strike "I didn't think you would mind" from your vocabulary.

1. Flush.

CONFLICT

As you go to school, eat, sleep, work, and have a social life all on the same campus with many of the same people, you'll probably have a few conflicts along the way. Don't let that throw you—it's natural. Fortunately, conflict can usually be resolved with little or no lasting damage. Conflict can also be a good teacher. Not all of life's lessons are learned in pleasant ways.

When Conflicts Arise

Don't try to find out who "started it." Instead, work together to find a solution.

Attack problems, not people. You should expect no winners and no losers—just solutions.

Listen to the other person and try to understand his or her concerns without judging. Listen with your heart as well as your head.

Tell the other person your concerns. Start your sentences with "I," not "You." Especially avoid, "You always," followed by a recap of past disputes. Focus on the future.

When you state the problem, **follow up with a positive suggestion** on how to solve it.

Know your objective. What do you want the other person to do? How do you want him or her to change behavior? What are your own needs? Be specific. Be ready to listen and to work on meeting needs.

Be respectful. Avoid name-calling and inflammatory words. Use language that will lead to the problem's solution rather than escalating the level of anger.

Talk with someone in authority, such as a resident assistant or resident director. They have been through this before.

BEING HEALTHY AND WISE

Your college years can be a wonderful time for you to establish a healthy lifestyle . . . for life. Wellness is not just the opposite of sickness. It is a comprehensive plan for living a full, healthy, and happy life. College life is action-packed. Too often students become wrapped up in classes, assignments, rehearsals, practices, meetings, and work, leaving little time for rest and relaxation.

Remember that to take advantage of everything an active college student wants to do, you have to take care of yourself and make sure your energy and overall health are good.

Issues to give some careful thought to include diet, exercise, sleep, stress, and drugs.

FOOD: HOW TO AVOID THE "FRESHMAN 15"

First-year students at college often experience a weight gain. That is partially because college life is often not too conducive to eating well. If you want to master the role and power of food in your life, start now. Here are some simple, commonsense tips to help you look better, feel better, and think better.

Manage the munchies. Beware of too much fast food, vending machines, and snacks. A little now and then is fine, but if you develop a habit of snacking, it will soon show.

"All you can eat" doesn't mean you have to eat all you can. Most college and university food plans allow you to eat as much as you want at each meal. But you don't have to sample everything or go back for seconds just because you can. Decide before you go to a meal how much you should eat.

Eat breakfast and avoid eating after supper. It's simple math. We burn more calories during the day than we do in the evening.

Eat a variety of foods. Too often college students eat the same types of food week in and week out. Over time, you will deplete your system of necessary nutrients. By varying your diet, you'll have more energy and better health.

Eat because you are hungry, not because you are bored or stressed out. Eat to live, don't live to eat. Listen to your stomach. When it's hungry, eat. When you are full, stop eating.

Drink lots of water throughout the day. This keeps your system running smoothly and carries impurities out of your body.

Maintain balance. This is the most important aspect of a person's diet. Protein, fruit, vegetables, fiber—you need it all in moderation. Your body can only function with the fuel you provide. Give yourself the advantage that comes from eating right.

Fortunately, most college food service providers now offer a wide variety of healthy options. They often provide nutritional information.

Eating disorders: anorexia (starving yourself) and bulimia (overeating and vomiting). Recent estimates indicate that as many as 2 million Americans suffer from eating disorders.

This is serious because such practices can kill you. Unfortunately, people with eating disorders usually won't admit it, even to themselves. If you face or a friend faces these problems, find someone you trust to talk to about it.

Eating disorders indicate problems with other issues—self-esteem, stress, or sometimes abuse.

You may also want to get more information on your own. Do an Internet search or contact the National Association of Anorexia Nervosa and Associated Disorders (ANAD) at P.O. Box 7, Highland Park, IL 60035 (847-831-3438). You may also want to contact the American Anorexia/Bulimia Association at 165 West 46th Street, No. 1108, New York, NY 10036 (212-575-6200).

You can also receive a free 17-page booklet on eating disorders by writing to the Consumer Information Catalog, P.O. Box 100, Pueblo, CO 81002. You can access this resource at http://www.pueblo.gsa.gov.

Reading and research won't be enough alone. Every college campus has a confidential counseling service with professionals who are trained to help. You can also check with the campus health office.

GETTING ENOUGH SLEEP: OTHER THAN IN CLASS

Humans need seven to nine hours of sleep regularly. You might think you are the exception to the rule, but in most cases you will pay a price in productivity and health if you deprive yourself of sleep. One of the best ways to ensure proper sleep is to establish a schedule and a daily routine that gives you time to study, work, enjoy recreation, and rest.

If you have a short night, catch a nap the next day and try to get to bed a little earlier than usual. Don't let your freedom to stay up entice you into poor habits that will ultimately hurt your grades and perhaps your health.

EXERCISE: GETTING AND STAYING IN SHAPE

You will probably have to take a physical education course or two to fulfill the general education requirements of your college. But those brief courses were never designed to meet your needs for exercise and fitness.

They were simply designed to introduce you to physical fitness as an ingredient of a healthy life.

A regular exercise program may be difficult for you if you are not athletic or not physically fit—all the more reason for you to establish an exercise program. Here are a few simple suggestions:

Walk everywhere you can. This simple activity will stimulate your metabolism and gradually help you become more active.

Join an intramural activity—volleyball, touch football, and so on. Exercise in a group activity is easier to continue over time.

Find a partner who will regularly exercise with you. This will provide accountability, encouragement, and support.

Take the stairs. This will give you mini workouts throughout the day. Don't think about it, don't even stop at the elevator, just do it.

Stretching for even a few minutes a day will help keep your body flexible.

Take care of your body—it is the only one you've got. When you are active you will feel better, sleep better, have more energy, be less susceptible to stress, and will stay more alert.

STRESS: WITHOUT DISTRESS

Stress is part of the fabric of university life. Some of the things that can cause stress while you are in college include:

- Pressure to get assignments done on time
- Tests
- Conflicts with your roommate
- Social pressures
- Financial problems
- Dating relationships (or lack thereof)

- Lack of sleep
- Illness
- Balancing school, work, and your social life

Stress is both a psychological and a physiological phenomenon, which can result in a host of symptoms, such as sleeplessness, irritability, mood swings, binge eating, apathy, dread, panic, headaches, high blood pressure, and more. It is a serious matter.

To counter the effects of stress and to avoid it when possible, you should:

- Limit the number of things you try to do in a semester. If your workload is extra heavy, take one less course.

- Adjust your mental attitude from being problem-oriented to seeing assignments and extra responsibilities as opportunities to compete and win.

- Get organized. Identify the most important tasks you have to complete. Prioritize them by importance and due dates. Start at the top of the list and stay with it. Check off each task as you accomplish it. This sense of accomplishment will give you energy and encouragement.

- Break a difficult task into smaller, manageable steps.

- Don't take on other peoples' problems. Learn to say no.

- No matter how busy you are, take a few moments to relax throughout the day.

- Go easy on the caffeine and sugar.

- Get some exercise.

- Get help. If you are really stuck, talk to your professor, your adviser, or a friend from class.

DRUGS: JUST SAY NO

You already know what you need to know. You simply have to decide where you stand and stick with it. Drugs, alcohol, and smoking are all part of youth culture and seem to be reinforced through the music and media of popular culture. Think of people (celebrities and sports heroes) who have lost everything they value due to the abuse of drugs.

SAFETY: A WORD TO THE WISE

College is about personal freedom and having fun, learning, and gaining new experiences. However, it also about taking more personal responsibility for your health and safety. Here are some tips:

Don't assume it could never happen to you. You could be the victim of a crime. Crimes happen every day on and around college campuses.

Ask about the crime statistics for the college or university you attend. Every school must publish and have on file for inspection a complete report of crimes that have occurred on campus.

Make sure your roommate or close friends know your schedule and where you are going. They should also know how to contact your parents in case of an emergency.

While living in a residence hall, **keep your room locked and your valuables out of sight** (my checkbook was stolen my first year!).

Don't leave valuables in your car.

Have a list of emergency numbers readily available (campus security, local police, fire, ambulance).

As much as possible, **walk in groups and stay in the light if you are out late.**

WHEN TWO'S COMPANY AND THE CAMPUS IS A CROWD

Dating is a wonderful part of college life—but don't take it too seriously, especially during your freshman year. You don't need to look at each member of the opposite gender as a potential girlfriend or boyfriend. Let friendships and relationships develop naturally, and dating will take care of itself.

Go out with groups of friends. This will give you an early chance to see how the person you might be attracted to acts around others. You may find out that he or she is not exactly what you had in mind after all.

When you do begin to date, take it slow. You'll have plenty of opportunities to be together. It is vital that you *get to know each other over time.*

THE STAGES OF A DATING RELATIONSHIP

The romance stage. This includes the initial rush of feelings for the other person. During this time you begin to get to know each other and build an emotional bond.

The power struggle stage. Differences begin to emerge, resulting in feelings of being less in control of the other person and often less in love. During this stage partners often feel competitive with one another.

The stability stage. Couples discover that the power struggle is not worth winning, that it is often a reflection of unresolved conflicts in themselves. They begin to understand that they don't always have to agree or want the same things. During this stage, couples begin to deepen their level of communication and trust.

The commitment stage. In this stage the feelings of love give way to the actions of love. Unselfishness and deep interest in the other person's best interests begin to dominate the relationship. This mutual commitment becomes the bedrock for a long-lasting relationship.

The cocreative stage. Here a oneness develops so that, although you retain your individuality and your own personality, as a couple you also develop an identity and personality.

Don't rush these stages, and don't be afraid of them. They are natural pathways to the development of intimacy and trust. Intimacy, which comes from opening ourselves more deeply to the other, is something we all crave and fear. *Dating takes work and respect and time.*

Also, don't feel that every time you are together has to be a big event. You can find lots of fun, interesting, and inexpensive dates. (Our first date was to church!)

- Attend a free concert or recital.
- Go to the gym together.
- Have a snowball fight or a walk on the beach.
- Play tennis.
- Take a hike.
- Browse a bookstore together.
- Attend a ball game.
- Walk to the Dairy Queen.

Sex?

Sex is good, not bad, but you need to know some important things: The trouble with sex as it is portrayed in the culture around you is that sex is seen as something to be pursued for its own sake, to achieve a momentary feeling or erotic sensation. When the importance and role of sex is distorted, we exploit others for selfish pleasure, and human sexuality suddenly loses its primary purpose, which is to create and sustain intimacy.

Sex is not a casual act, not just a physical act. It carries with it strong emotional and psychological imprinting. This is one reason the Bible clearly reserves sexual relationships for those who are married.

The time to make your sexual decisions is *long before* you are sitting alone with your date in a parked car. Set limits and feel free to talk with your dating partner about how you feel and what you expect. It is very easy to get entangled sexually simply by "letting nature take its course." The price for sexual promiscuity is high. Pregnancy, disease, guilt, memories, distrust, and emotional scars can all result from one careless moment.

Date Rape: A Word of Caution

Girls, it can happen, so don't be naive. Nice guys can turn out to be not so nice. Say NO! and mean it. If he persists, tell him you will report him to campus authorities and to the police if he doesn't back off. You can't be tentative if the guy really intends to harm you.

Guys, like it or not, no means no. To disregard that warning is to commit a crime: sexual harassment or rape.

OTHER CAMPUS LIFE STRATEGIES

COLLEGE SPORTS

There is something satisfying and even therapeutic about being involved in sports. Whether it's soccer, basketball, running, swimming, or any other such activity you enjoy, simply participating can be a life-enhancing decision.

Being involved in sports affects you on many levels:

- It is a physical outlet.
- It gives you a chance to improve your health and coordination.
- It gives the opportunity to take your mind off assignments, to enjoy the moment and clear your mind.
- It is an avenue to make friends.
- It gives you an emotional outlet to cheer and be passionate and enthusiastic.

You don't have to be a varsity athlete to participate in college sports. Most campuses have a full range of intramural athletics. If, however, you do participate in varsity intercollegiate athletics, you need to know being a college athlete means making a year-round commitment. You will need to be mentally and emotionally prepared to balance a full academic load and manage the demands and pressures of athletic competition.

The biggest mistakes college athletes make are not spending enough time on their schoolwork and not managing their free time correctly. Always keep a strong focus on your grades. If they go down, you could be sidelined.

VOLUNTEERING

One great lesson of life is to learn to give rather than get, to serve others. College students can make a difference in lots of wonderful ways. There will be many opportunities available to you.

- Tutoring, either on campus or through a local school
- Helping the Salvation Army
- Getting involved through a local church
- Volunteering at a nursing home or daycare center
- Being a big brother or big sister
- Working with Habitat for Humanity
- Going on a missions trip
- Joining campus efforts to serve the poor
- Providing counseling and tax preparation for those in need

Volunteering your time and energies will help you nearly as much as it helps the person or cause you are working with.

Something about service work is gratifying. Plus, you can volunteer with friends. What a great way to spend time together—having fun and being helpful.

MISCELLANEOUS TIPS IN NO PARTICULAR ORDER

- If you have to work, remember the good jobs go fast, so start looking early.
- Makeup tests are generally much harder.
- Watch the eyes. If a professor looks down at his or her notes before speaking, the next sentence is probably important.
- One credit card is enough, in fact it is too often more than enough.
- Save your quarters for the laundry.

- If you took a language in high school and plan to continue with it in college, do it early. The longer you wait, the more you will forget from the past.
- Studying in bed is an illusion. After 15 minutes, you're history.
- Keep your eye on your towel when you go to take a shower.
- Correct your mistakes when you get the test back. A corrected test is a great study aid for the final exam.
- Get help as soon as you need it. Problems don't get better on their own.
- Summer is a good time to take a course to either catch up or get ahead.
- Don't let yourself get behind.
- Be yourself.
- Speak and smile.

Part 5

THE SPIRITUAL ADVENTURE

But one thing I do: Forgetting what is behind and straining toward what is ahead, I press on toward the goal to win the prize for which God has called me heavenward in Christ Jesus.

—Phil. 3:13-14

Building on a Firm Foundation

The building sits on two city blocks and rises more than one-quarter of a mile into the sky. Its 110 stories comprise 4.5 million square feet of office and commercial space. The Sears Tower, in the heart of Chicago, breaks the plane of the horizon when it is still more than 20 miles away.

Two thousand construction men worked around the clock for nearly 3 years to build it. And for more than 20 years the Sears Tower stood as the world's tallest building. It is still the tallest building in all of the Americas.

Not many folk can fully grasp everything involved in engineering and constructing such a massive building, but one thing is sure: when the actual construction got underway, the first direction the workmen went was not up but down.

Before a building can reach for the sky, it must be anchored, first, on a firm foundation. How true that is of life itself—before you build a life, you must first determine the foundation. Foundations are fundamental.

Among all of the other things involved in going to college, the most important aspect is that you will be much more "on your own" in a spiritual way than ever before. Being away from home and in the midst of a college environment gives you the chance and offers you the challenge to mature spiritually as well as socially and academically.

During your college years, you must decide, without the daily influence of parents, what you believe about God, about the Bible, and about your own spiritual condition. Sometimes it takes leaving home to get us ready to really come to know God personally.

Did you ever have an elementary school art class in which you were handed a piece of paper with an outline of some picture, perhaps a tree and a house—and then you were instructed to color in between the lines? Your teacher may have given you a stern reminder to "stay inside the lines."

Week after week you followed the same procedures. Your only freedom for creativity was in choosing which of the eight colors in the Crayola box to use. If your crayon slipped, or through carelessness you wandered outside the lines, your "artwork" was unacceptable.

Often, even in godly homes, children are instructed in religion in the same way elementary children are instructed in art. They are handed someone else's outline and are told to stay within the lines.

Have you ever felt that way? Everyone is expecting you to live his or her Christian life. God does not want you to simply copy someone else's experience—He wants to lead you in creating your own religious experience; drawing your own lines, in partnership with Him—lines you can live within with integrity and comfort.

As you think about finding yourself spiritually, remember you'll find no success without God and no lasting failure with Him. A mature faith in God is not a rabbit's foot, something you have just for "good luck." Believing in God and committing yourself to His will is not a parachute to use only in emergencies. Finding a personal faith in God is a fundamental part of deciding who you are and what you ultimately believe.

If you are already a Christian . . . going to college will help you mature spiritually. But college may also test your faith in some new ways.

• Your added freedom and autonomy may bring temptations that you might not have experienced yet.

• You will meet other Christian students who do not believe exactly as you do. They come from different denominations and faith traditions. All of this will force you to sift carefully through differing opinions. You may have to work a little harder to decide what you really believe.

• You will encounter some students (and depending on where you go to college, even some professors) who will openly challenge your Christian commitment.

If you are not a Christian . . . going to college will give you the opportunity to come to faith in Christ on your own, when you are ready.

• No one will force you to go to church.

• Only you can decide to accept Christ and let Him lead you as you set the course for your future.

• You will face new temptations and the consequences of your responses to those temptations.

• Remember, you don't have to understand it all, you don't have to be free of doubt or questions to have faith. But you must choose, God or no God. The moment a person comes to faith in God becomes **the defining moment of self-identity in his or her life.**

The Bible calls you to faith; not faith in faith—but faith in God, the Creator, the One who loves you. But you, alone, must decide. On the one hand is the call of culture. It is the call to conform, the call of the crowd. On the other hand there is the call of Christ—"follow Me."

At the end of the day, when all is said and done, when

you total all of your life's experiences—the accomplish-
ments, disappointments, and successes—you will find
the most important issue in life is not "Where did you go
to college?" or "What was your major?" The most important thing will be "What did you do with Jesus Christ?"
Did you believe? Were you willing to accept Him as Savior
and Lord? Or did you go your own way?

You must decide . . .

Is the Bible false?

Does God really exist?

Did this world, with all of its intricacies and miracles,
just happen, or is a purpose at work here?

Are you nothing more than an animal?

Is every Christian wrong and the church mistaken?

All of us must answer those questions. **And remember, not to decide *is* to decide.** Because you are a person
of free will, you alone must decide what you believe.

The world around us and the society in which we live
has done about all it can do to destroy faith. The assault
on Christianity has sometimes been subtle through the
slow but steady erosion of truth and morality, or through
marginalizing and neutralizing the message of the gospel
from daily life. At other times the attack on Christian faith
has been much more obvious.

We are, in many ways, part of a society that has been
numbed by evil. Many young people, good kids, don't
seem to be able to distinguish right from wrong. They
have gone the way of the world that believes that it is all
relative—there are no real rights and wrongs.

You are living in a culture that has been

• seduced by false reason,

• overwhelmed by science and technology and

• confronted with suffering and injustice

All of this can be used to call the Christian faith into
question.

Even so, have faith in God, don't be afraid to believe.
Faith will take nothing from you.

- It doesn't make you less of a person.
- It doesn't rob you of your free will or your personality.
- It doesn't destroy your sense of pleasure.

To believe is to turn on the light in a dark world. If you live your whole life in a dimly lit cave, you think the shadows are reality. But if you ever walk out into the light, the true light, and see the world as it really is, you never want to live in the cave again.

Let the new level of freedom that comes to you when you go to college become an avenue to God. Let your doubts be a ladder to faith—not a barrier.

The truth is you were either created by God or you are a tiny bit of living matter that has mutated across the eons until there was you. If that is the case—then eat, drink, and be merry, for nothing else matters very much.

But if, on the other hand, you are created by God—as a living, immortal soul—then that changes everything. You have purpose and meaning and value. Who are you? You have to decide, and you must live and die with that decision.

As you deal with that question, don't be afraid to risk believing that you are in fact a child of God and to start, even now, living out your true purpose and inheritance.

The call of Christ is to **"Come, follow me!"** And that is a step of faith. It means that . . .

You choose to believe in the God of the Bible (after all, the Book is either true or false, you have to decide).

You accept Jesus' will as the supreme authority for life. You see at a point in life, a person must turn faith into action. At some time, if we are going to follow Christ, we must follow Him. *Follow* is a beautiful word; it speaks of guidance and companionship and progress.

The call of Christ in our lives means we accept God's will as the supreme authority for life. Have you done that; have you accepted God's will as your will?

The call of Christ also means that . . .

We accept the character of Jesus as the supreme ideal for life. That's what following is all about—it is to walk in the steps of the Master. He is what we should be. Every believer should be able to say, "I am becoming more like Jesus as I follow Him." We take His word seriously. We seek to find how Christ might respond in a given situation. "What would Jesus do?" we ask.

Unfortunately, some who say they follow Jesus are not very Christlike. This is serious business. A personal commitment to follow Jesus must be reflected in how we live our lives.

Coming to a personal faith in Christ is the challenge of a lifetime. In some ways, college is the best place and the best time to make your personal commitment. It won't get any easier once you graduate and move fully into the world.

Part 6

FINAL THOUGHTS FOR YOUR GREAT ADVENTURE

To educate a man in mind and not in morals is to educate a menace to society.
—Theodore Roosevelt

PREPARE FOR AN EXTRAORDINARY TRIP

A generation ago, Lloyd Douglas wrote a book, *The Magnificent Obsession*. He tells the story of a man named Robert Merrick, a rich, young, self-centered fellow who is out sailing his father's yacht on a large, secluded lake. Merrick has been drinking heavily and is carelessly knocked overboard by a boom that shifts suddenly and strikes him from behind.

Rescued at the point of death, Merrick is pulled out of the water and taken to the lakeside home of Dr. Wayne Hudson, a well-known and beloved surgeon. Upon arrival, Merrick is immediately hooked up to a respirator kept at the house for the doctor's use.

Now at the same time, the doctor, who was not home through all of this, but out swimming in the water, suddenly suffers cramps, also goes under, and he, too, is rescued. He is rushed to his own home but the respirator is not available, because it is already being used on the young man, Robert Merrick. The doctor dies.

When Merrick is taken to the hospital to recover further, he overhears one nurse saying to another, "What a tragedy that a great man who saved lives should be lost, and this fellow, who never did any good for anybody, should be saved."

For the first time, Merrick begins to see himself for the

self-centered, spoiled, and uncaring person he is. In his mind is born a dream of what he really could do, of who he might really be with this second chance at life.

What a thought!

This individual gains a new perspective on life, a new beginning, as he realizes another man more deserving than he has died so that he might live. It is as if Merrick has been born again.

This experience fills him with an obsession to live his life to honor the one who had saved him. This focus propels him and guides him for the rest of his life, until he completes his mission of becoming a great surgeon to carry on the work cut short by Dr. Hudson's death.

It's a great story—but of course it is more than just a story. It is a metaphor, a parable, a mirror in which you can see yourself. You, along with every other person, are driven by some set of values and priorities. These may not take the shape of an obsession, but something is at work within each of us, something that determines the direction and passion of our lives.

What potential there is, if during your college years you come to the place where you lose yourself in some high and noble mission; when you give yourself to the magnificent obsession of living to the glory of the one who died for us.

Consider the following verses from the Bible. These words were originally written by the apostle Paul to the church in the ancient city of Philippi. He identifies himself as a man driven by a magnificent obsession of his own. He declares, in Phil. 3:10: "I want to know Christ and the power of his resurrection." And then he says: "One thing I do: Forgetting what is behind and straining toward what is ahead, I press on toward the goal to win the prize for which God has called me heavenward in Christ Jesus" (vv. 13-14).

Paul has a mission. He has something to live for that has transformed him. And he is persuaded that this is true for all who belong to Christ.

In the movie *Chariots of Fire,* the Master of Gonville and Caius College at Cambridge, England, greets his entering freshman class with these words: "Let me exhort you, let each of you discover where your true chance of greatness lies . . . seize this chance, rejoice in it, and let no power or persuasion deter you in your task."

This is good advice. You are to sift through the many options in life and choose the one that most fits you, then give yourself wholeheartedly to it.

What motivates you?

What drives you to succeed?

What do you most care about?

MOTIVATION: FIND IT OR FAIL

Motivation will help you move from who you are to who you might become. This factor, which determines success or failure both in school and in life, is sometimes elusive, even hard to define. Motivation is a combination of interest, ambition, values, and desire.

The power of motivation lies in striving to be the best you can be, and that must take root within your own mind and will. Being genuinely motivated helps you do what you should do now, so you can gain what you want later.

An old legend tells of an American Indian boy who found an eagle's egg but could not find the nest. So the boy carefully laid the egg in the nest of one of his family's chickens.

The eagle hatched along with a brood of chickens and grew up with them—thinking it was a chicken and doing only what the chickens did. It scratched in the dirt for seeds and insects to eat. It never flew more than a short distance. After all, chickens don't really fly.

Then one day, when the eagle was grown, it saw a magnificent bird far above in the sky. Riding with graceful majesty on powerful wind currents, it soared with scarcely a beat of its broad wings.

"What a beautiful bird!" said the eagle to one of the chickens. "What is it?"

"That's an eagle, the chief of birds," the chicken replied. "But don't give it a second thought. You could never fly like that."

So the eagle never gave it a second thought, never rose beyond the brief thrashing of wings and the flurry of feathers. It grew old and died thinking it was a chicken—when all along the way it carried within itself the making of an eagle.[6]

Don't settle for less than your full potential. Sure, college will be difficult sometimes, but you can make it.

> *Do you not know?*
> *Have you not heard?*
> *The LORD is the everlasting God,*
> *the Creator of the ends of the earth.*
> *He will not grow tired or weary,*
> *and his understanding no one can fathom.*
> *He gives strength to the weary*
> *and increases the power of the weak.*
> *Even youths grow tired and weary,*
> *and young men stumble and fall;*
> *but those who hope in the LORD*
> *will renew their strength.*
> *They will soar on wings like eagles;*
> *they will run and not grow weary,*
> *they will walk and not be faint.*
> (Isa. 40:28-31)

---

6. William Armstrong and M. Willard Lampe II, *Study Tactics* (Hauppauge, N.Y.: Barron's Educational Series, Inc., 1983), 260.

You can make it if you start with the end in mind, if you take full advantage of the resources and people available and willing to help you, if you make your choices carefully, and most of all, if you will let God be part of your college adventure.

Perhaps, in the course of time, after you finish college, you may forget much of what you learned during those days: the mathematical equations, the dates, names, and places from history, the chemical formulas, the intricacies of a fine sonnet; if not used, you may forget these in time.

You will probably forget the combination to your mailbox, your student ID number, and your E-mail password. You may forget some of the names and faces of your college classmates—and in the big picture of life, all of that forgetting may not matter too much.

But if you forget God, if you forget the One who died for you, if you let your life get cluttered and crowded and cramped; if you lose your way spiritually, then no other amount of remembering will make much difference.

As you start your college adventure, ask yourself this question, "Are you drifting or are you pursuing some worthy goal?" Remember, "There is no failure quite like success without God."

Do you have purpose and focus in your life? Is it sufficient for a lifetime? Where will you be when you get to where you're headed?

Paul says, "I want to know Christ and [His] power . . . forgetting what is behind and straining toward what is ahead."

Don't just live—get a life. Let your college years play a vital part of finding your magnificent obsession.

GLOSSARY

Accreditation—Schools and individual programs (nursing, teacher education, and so on) are all evaluated by outside groups who visit the campus and provide an official evaluation of the quality of the school or program. Students should check carefully to make sure the college and major they choose has been "accredited."

ACT—The American College Test is used by many colleges and universities to assess a student's academic preparation for college. The ACT is divided into four sections: an English section, a math section, a reading section, and a science reasoning section. A score of 1 to 36 is given for each section, as well as an overall composite score.

Advanced placement—AP tests are administered by the college board and focus on a single subject, such as history, science, English, foreign languages, and more. Achieving a minimum score on a "placement test" allows you to enroll in a more advanced course.

Alma mater—Alma mater is the school, college, or university you attended. The term *alma mater* is Latin and literally means "nourishing or fostering mother." The idea is that one's college or university helps a person come of age; it fosters and nourishes him or her and thus becomes an alma mater. The term is also used to describe the school song.

Alumni—College graduates. An alumnus is a man; an alumna is a woman; alumni (-ae) is the plural.

Assessment—A way of determining how much students are actually learning. This is generally done by administering pretests and posttests.

Associate degree—A degree granted by a junior or community college after two years of study.

Audit—To take a course for no credit, to sit in on lectures and do the assignments for the pleasure of learning, not for a grade or credit.

Baccalaureate—A four-year college degree, also known as a **bachelor's degree**.

Block courses—Courses offered for one-half of a semester or academic term. Generally the course meets twice as often during that time to accommodate the shorter schedule.

Board (Governing Board, Board of Trustees, Regents)—The governing board of the college/university. The board hires the president who, in turn, gives oversight, leadership, and supervision to the university operations and reports directly to the board for the administration of the school.

Bursar—A college treasurer or business officer. Student accounts are sometimes handled by the bursar's office.

Carrel—A study booth in the library. Usually reserved for graduate students or upper division commuting students.

Catalog—The official booklet of a college or university that tells the history, mission, organizational structure of the school, along with a description of course offerings, institutional requirements, policies, and procedures.

Chancellor—The term is used to designate the president of the university, usually in large, multicampus universities.

CLEP—College Level Examination Program that provides "credit by examination." If a student can demonstrate mastery of a subject through advance testing, he or she can earn academic credit without taking a given course. It is a great way to free up your schedule and save money on tuition. For examination information call: 609-771-7865 or visit **www.collegeboard.org.**

Cognate—Required courses that are related but outside your major.

Comprehensive exam—An examination that covers all of the material presented in a class up to that point as compared to a unit exam, which covers only a portion of the material studied in a given class.

Consortium—An association of schools working collectively on common interests and shared programs.

Convocation—Literally, the term means "calling together." It describes formal campuswide gatherings, usually at the beginning or end of the academic year.

Credit hour—The basic unit in which academic credit is awarded. It generally corresponds to the number of hours a class meets per week during the semester. A three-credit-hour course would meet three times a week for an hour (50 minutes) each time.

Curriculum—The course offerings for a degree program, major or minor.

Dean—A university official who generally has academic oversight, such as the dean of the college or the dean of the business school. The term is also applied to nonacademic administrators such as dean of students.

Dean's list—A listing of students who have excelled academically during a semester. The list is made up of those who attained a minimum GPA. It is somewhat like the high school Honor Roll.

Directed study—A directed study course is offered on an individual basis by special arrangement with a professor. These courses are not common but are occasionally arranged when, for extenuating circumstances, a student cannot take the course at the regular time.

Distance education—Courses and/or entire degree programs delivered to off-campus students via one or more distance communication technologies (Internet, satellite, video, and so on). Often on-campus students can participate in a course that either originates on campus and is then transmitted to others, or take a course in a campus classroom that has originated somewhere else.

Drop/add—To officially drop or enroll in a class. Generally a student may add or drop a course without penalty until a certain point in the academic term. Once you sign up for a course, you must officially drop it if you do not wish to complete the course. If you just drop out and quit going to class without completing the "drop" procedures, you will fail the course and it will become part of your official transcript.

Elective—A course not required to complete a major or minor course of study. Electives may count toward the general education requirements or may be taken simply for fun.

Emeritus—An honorary rank bestowed upon a retired professor or administrative officer.

Endowment—Funds permanently held in trust by a school or foundation that generate annual revenue from the investment of those funds. A portion of the annual revenue is then used to provide scholarships and cover operational expenses and provide money for buildings. Most endowments are restricted to one of those specific purposes.

Fees—The *fine print* of college costs. Fees are charges for things not covered by room and board and tuition. Special fees may be assessed for private lessons, use of laboratories, parking, technology, or general student activities.

Freshman—A first-year student. Look in the mirror, it's you!

GED—General equivalency exam taken by individuals who did not graduate from high school. Thus, passing the exam is the equivalent of having completed high school.

General education requirements (Gen. Ed.)—Courses in the liberal arts and sciences, which are required of all students for graduation. One-fourth to one-third of your courses will be taken to fulfill these requirements.

GPA—Grade point average, which is figured by assigning a numerical value to a traditional letter grade. A = 4, B = 3, C = 2, D = 1. A person who makes straight A's would thus have a perfect 4.0 GPA.

Grant—Money awarded for college tuition and expenses, without the expectation of repayment.

Independent study—See directed study.

Interdisciplinary—Involving two or more academic fields of study. Some courses overlap and are listed in the course offerings of more than one department. Some courses are team-taught by professors from different departments. A course in music history, for example, involves both the study of music and of world history.

Intern, internship—A student or recent graduate who works in an apprentice relationship to learn the real-life applications of a given field of study. Internships can be either paid or nonpaid.

Junior standing—An academic designation signifying that a student has completed approximately one-half of the required credit hours for graduation and has declared a major. Some courses are restricted only to students with junior standing.

Liberal arts—Academic college courses providing general knowledge and comprising the arts, humanities, natural sciences, and social sciences. A college that requires a core curriculum of courses that are to be taken by every student, regardless of major, is called a liberal arts college.

Lower/upper division—These terms designate course offerings on the basis of whether, on the average, the course is taken during the first two years of college (lower division) or during the last two years (upper division). Courses are generally assigned a three-digit number. The 100s are for first-year courses, 200s for the second-year courses, and so on.

Major—This term is used to describe or designate your primary course of study, that is, business, biology, art, and so on. There is generally a special set of courses and a minimum number of academic hours one takes to complete a major. Some students will complete a "double major," which simply means that he or she has fulfilled the course requirements in two areas of study.

Matriculate—This is a big term that simply means to enroll in a college or university. Once you have enrolled, you have matriculated. It comes from a Latin term that means "list." So to be enrolled is to be on the list of students.

Minor—This is a concentration of courses one takes as a secondary pursuit to his or her major. For example, a person might major in business and minor in communications.

Natural sciences—These are courses that deal with the natural world (such as biology, chemistry, geology). This is in contrast to the "social sciences," such as sociology, psychology, social work, history, political science.

Oral exam—This means that an examination is given by a professor asking a student questions and getting verbal answers rather than written answers. It is conversational and direct. Oral exams are not often given but are sometimes used when a student has to make up for a missed exam or if the class is particularly small.

Orientation—A designated time, following admission, for new students to visit the campus, meet key personnel, receive instructions, be assigned an adviser, preregister for courses, and make housing arrangements. Often orientations are held once or twice during the summer months or just before the opening of school.

Pass/fail—A standard of course evaluation other than the granting of a specific grade. Instead, a student either simply passes or fails. Sometimes this system is used for subjects like physical education courses.

Practicum—A course of study devoted to practical experience in a particular field.

Preprofessional programs—College degree programs designed specifically to help students planning for graduate school admission in areas such as medicine or law.

Preregistration—A process of declaring your intention to register for a particular course or set of courses. This is generally done near the end of one semester for the next semester. Preregistration is followed at the beginning of the next semester by formal registration as classes begin.

Prerequisite—A course that is required before taking another course. For example, *Introduction to Business* might be a prerequisite for *Business Law*.

Probation—Academic probation is a trial period or condition of a student who is being permitted to continue in school in an effort to demonstrate his or her ability to complete the work satisfactorily, or is permitted to continue in school under the restriction that grades must improve. Social probation may be administered as part of campus discipline following an infraction or a series of infractions of the campus code of conduct.

Proctor—A person appointed to keep watch over student examinations.

Professor/professorial rank—College teachers are known and addressed as professors. There are various designations (ranks) depending upon experience and education. These range from instructor to assistant professor to associate professor to full professor. After a professor retires from active teaching, he or she may be designated as professor emeritus.

Provost—Generally, the second highest ranking administrative officer of the university. This person oversees the academic program and gives leadership and supervision to the university in the absence of the president.

R.A. (resident assistant or adviser)—Usually an upper-class student who lives in the residence hall to provide supervision and assistance to students.

Reference room—A section of the library where reference works, encyclopedias, manuals, bibliographies, and dictionaries are kept. Reference works cannot usually be checked out; you must use them in the library.

Remedial courses—Courses designed specifically to improve poor skills in a specified field. On occasion a remedial course is required for a student to enter a course of study.

ROTC—Reserve Officers Training Corp.

Sabbatical—An extended leave of absence granted to a professor to be used for study and rest. Professors may be away for a semester or a year on a sabbatical leave.

SAT—The Scholastic Aptitude Test. This exam is used to measure a student's readiness for college and is often a basis upon which admission is granted or scholarships are awarded. The SAT is divided into two sections: a main section and a verbal section. 1,600 points are possible, 800 from each section.

Scholarship—The qualities, skills, or attainments of a scholar. The term is also used for a gift of money or other aid award (without the expectation of repayment) to help a student attend college.

Seminar—A small class designated for upper-division and graduate students. The emphasis in a seminar is generally on independent research and class discussion.

Social sciences—The academic areas of study that deal with human personality and interaction: sociology, social work, criminal justice, business, history, political science, family and consumer science, psychology.

Socratic method—The use of questions, as employed by the Greek philosopher Socrates, to develop a latent idea in the mind of a student.

Syllabus—The outline of a course, prepared by a professor, which details the subjects to be covered, the books and resources used, and the assignments required.

Testing out—Getting a course requirement waived by taking a test and demonstrating your mastery of the course material. See CLEP.

Thesis—The subject or key idea of a composition or essay. Also a formal paper based on original research, especially one presented by a candidate for a degree.

Transcript—The formal record of earned academic credit. A copy is permanently on file in the registrar's office, which provides copies upon request to employers and graduate schools.

Transfer student—One who has switched (transferred) from one school to another.

Tuition—The charge or fee for instruction. Tuition is generally figured on a rate of so much per credit hour.